Propertius
Modernist Poet of Antiquity

D. Thomas Benediktson

Southern Illinois University Press
Carbondale and Edwardsville

Printed in the United States of America
Edited by Carol A. Burns
Designed by Jody Dyer Jasinski
Production supervised by Natalia Nadraga
92 91 90 89 4 3 2 1

Grateful acknowledgment is made to quote the following works: "Arethusa to Lycotas," reprinted by Faber and Faber Ltd. from *Day by Day* by Robert Lowell and reprinted by permission of Farrar, Straus, and Giroux, Inc., "Arethusa to Lycotas" from *Day by Day* by Robert Lowell. Copyright ©1975, 1976, 1977 by Robert Lowell; "Poem VII," from *Homage to Sextus Propertius* reprinted by Faber and Faber Ltd. from *Collected Shorter Poems* by Ezra Pound and Ezra Pound, *Personae*. Copyright ©1926 by Ezra Pound. Reprinted by permission of New Directions Publishing Corporation; Selections from *The Poems of Sextus Propertius,* trans. Constance Carrier, Indiana University Press, 1963; Philodemus, 5.112, reprinted by permission of the publishers and the Loeb Classical Library from *The Greek Anthology,* trans. W. R. Paton, Cambridge, Mass.: Harvard University Press; London: William Heinemann, Copyright © 1916–18.

Library of Congress Cataloging-in-Publication Data

Benediktson, D. Thomas, 1951–
Propertius: modernist poet of antiquity / by D. Thomas Benediktson.
p. cm.
Bibliography: p.
Includes index.
ISBN 0-8093-1453-3
1. Propertius, Sextus—Criticism and interpretation.
2. Propertius, Sextus—Influence. 3. Modernism (Literature)
4. Imagist poetry—History and criticism. I. Title.
PA6646.B4 1989
874'.01—dc 19

The paper used in this publication meets the minimum requirements of American National Standard for Information Sciences—Permanence of Paper for Printed Library Materials, ANSI Z39.48–1984. ♾

For My Family

The philologists have so succeeded in stripping the classics of interest that I have already had more than one reader who has asked me, "Who was Propertius?" As for my service to classical scholarship, presumably nil, I shall be quite content if I induce a few Latinists really to look at the text of Propertius instead of swallowing an official "position" and then finding what the textbooks tell them to look for.

Ezra Pound, *The New Age*

Contents

Preface

This book is the product both of the classicist environment in which I was educated and of the modernist environment in which I teach. Parts of the book go back to my research at The University of Texas at Austin, although the conception and plan of the work grew while reading Propertius with two graduate students in modern letters, Curtis Cottrell and (now Professor) Michael Warner, at The University of Tulsa. I realized in discussions with these students that Propertius' poetry is necessarily read quite differently by modernists than by classicists. The problems which became insurmountable to a Housman are trivial and perhaps not even apparent to a Pound. This book is addressed to both audiences, to those who read as Housmans and to those who read as Pounds.

I owe thanks to many friends and colleagues who have contributed to the completion of this book: Professors Karl Galinsky, Barbara K. Gold, M. Gwyn Morgan, William R. Nethercut, and Carl A. Rubino. Earlier drafts of part or all of the manuscript were read and improved by Professors Gold, Rubino, and Warner as well as by Professor Norman S. Grabo, Dean Susan Resneck Parr, Professor Ludwig Koenen, and my wife, Caroline Benediktson. Professor J. P. Sullivan also suggested many improvements and corrected numerous errors. I would also like to thank the editorial staff of Southern Illinois University Press, especially Robert S. Phillips and Carol Burns, for continued help of various kinds. The project was supported by a summer fellowship in 1984 granted by The Henry Kendall College of Arts and Sciences, The University of Tulsa, and by a research grant from The University of Tulsa Faculty Research Program of the Office of Research in fall 1983. The college and the Office of Research also jointly contributed funds for manuscript production and defrayed the costs of obtaining permissions to quote copyrighted materials. I would in addition like to thank Alberta Frost and the entire staff of the Interlibrary Loan Department of MacFarlin Library, The University of Tulsa, who made it possible to do most of the research while eating home cooking.

Finally, I would like to thank my family for their continued advice and support throughout.

1
The Propertian Ring

Interest in Sextus Propertius in the twentieth century has been immense. He has been translated by Ezra Pound and Robert Lowell, apparently imitated by James Joyce, and studied and commented upon by Benedetto Croce. These are some of the prominent names of twentieth-century modernism, and no other ancient author has elicited such attention. If the early Middle Ages were the *aetas Vergiliana* and the eleventh century the *aetas Ovidiana*, the twentieth century might be the *aetas Propertiana*.

For all of this popularity among nonclassicists, classicists have not known quite what to make of Propertius. Classical scholars have not even been able to accomplish what seems to be the basic task in the study of an ancient author, that is, to determine his text. Standard editions of Catullus or Ovid vary little, but in Propertius lines are transposed, poems are divided in various ways or connected to adjoining poems, and lacunae are printed here and there. A popular aphorism in Propertian textual criticism is "quot editores, tot Propertii" ("however many editors there are, there are that many Propertii"). Even the novice reader of Propertius is expected to be textual critic and literary critic rolled into one. It is no wonder that very few graduate students in classics, and almost no undergraduates, have ever read him.

There is consensus on one thing—Propertius' talent. Most moderns would agree that he was the greatest of the Roman elegists, a judgment the ancients did not share. Quintilian thought Tibullus the best, adding that "there are some who prefer Propertius" (*Institutio Oratoria* 10.1.93). But a great many modern studies of poems like 1.1, 1.3, and 4.7 have shown that Propertius was capable of far greater work, to our taste at least, than was Tibullus. This demonstration has aggravated the problem. If these few poems are so good, why are so many others, again to the taste of the modern classicist, completely unreadable? Recent studies of Propertius have given us tools to appreciate certain aspects of his writing, but how can we appreciate his corpus as a whole? Why would a poet seemingly obsessed with the mathematical balance of lines within poems and of poems within books leave us with Book II in its present form, which Richardson, several years before producing his edition and commentary, referred to as a "mass of spaghetti" (qtd. in Sullivan, *Propertius* 7)?

Nineteenth-century editors suggested that the text must have suffered large-scale damage in the Middle Ages. Lachmann, early in the nineteenth century, had suggested that Propertius wrote five books rather than the four of the manuscripts, and that our Book II was a compilation of two books (II and III of the five-book edition). (Since Müller adopted this numbering system in his Teubner text, students of Pound will be familiar with this chaotic situation.) According to this hypothesis the damage to the corpus would have occurred when Book I, which evidently circulated alone in antiquity under the title "Monobiblos," was added to the last four books. In recent studies the five-book explanation has been coming back into vogue (Skutsch, "Book"; Sullivan, *Propertius* 6–8; Margaret Hubbard 41; but not Papanghelis 140–44), and the recent editions of Richardson and Hanslik show that the trend among editors is toward increasing emendation and transposition. But are these trends justified? The evidence in the medieval grammarians for the division of Book II has been shown to be negligible, and as even Skutsch admits, judgments as to damage of the text are "subjective" ("Book" 230; cf. Menes).[1] An examination and consideration of the text as transmitted in the manuscripts and an assessment of the corpus as a whole are long overdue.

Often when classical texts show the kind of variety seen in the editions of Propertius, the fault lies in the manuscript tradition. The tradition for Propertius is weak and still controversial, but that is not the difficulty. After one of the most thorough examinations of the manuscript tradition of any author and after the hypothetical creation of an entirely new family of manuscripts, Butrica (*Manuscript*) offers 238 lines of sample text that are not very different from the equivalent lines in Barber's Oxford Classical Text. A fair number of variant readings and several transpositions are accepted and one poem is divided in a new place, but these are mostly emendations. Only four readings at variance with Barber's are supported by the readings of Butrica's new family (*X*), and these are all in 4.11, where *N*, a major manuscript related to *X*, is lost. If Butrica's ideas gain acceptance, the critical apparatus of future editions of Propertius will be radically different, but the text itself will be influenced little. Conservative editions will continue to resemble the Oxford Classical Texts of Phillimore and Barber, moderate editions those of Richardson and Hanslik, and radical ones that of Richmond. The division of poems, the transposition of lines and the postulation of lacunae will continue to occur at editors' whims, not on manuscript authority.

If we wish to see why classicists have had so much trouble with Propertius, there is no better starting point than A. E. Housman, who worked extensively with Propertius and still has a reputation for being one of the best Latinists and textual critics of the past two centuries. At Oxford, Housman failed his examination for honors in "Greats" (philosophy and history) because he had spent his time studying the literary authors he liked, such as Propertius, rather than those which were to appear on the examination.[2] He withdrew from school, worked for several years in the Patent Office, and spent much of his spare time studying the text and manuscript tradition of Propertius. This study resulted in Housman's first major publications, without academic affiliation, a brilliant (and still important) set of articles entitled "Emendationes Propertianae," "Note on Emendations of Propertius," and "The Manuscripts of Propertius" (*Papers*). These articles earned him his first academic position as Chair of Latin at the University of London. "Emendationes Propertianae" offers many new emendations and transpositions. "The Manuscripts of Propertius" was the first balanced and "scientific" study of the manuscript tradition, and although the conclusions are no longer accepted today, the work stands as a masterpiece in English classical studies. Housman is known today for his editions of Lucan and Manilius, but Propertius launched his career.

In spite of all this work on Propertius, Housman was unable to produce an edition. He prepared a manuscript that Macmillan rejected, and when he died Housman had the manuscript burned. Especially in transpositions the edition would have differed from most. On poem 3.7, for example, printed by Barber without a single transposition, Housman wrote: "The verses of this elegy should be arranged thus: 1–10, 43–66, 17 and 18, 11–16, 67–70, 25–32, 37 and 38, 35 and 36, 19 and 20, 33 and 34, 21–4, 39–42, 71 and 72" (*Papers* 35). He gives neither a justification for such revisions nor an explanation of how the text became disfigured. If the edition had appeared, Propertian studies would be different today.

It does not bode well for Propertian studies that Housman, a brilliant textual critic and a practicing poet as well, could not produce a presentable text of Propertius. We need to ask why. The explanation, I believe, can be found in the analysis of many of his transpositions. The following poem is a case in point:

multum in amore fides, multum constantia prodest
    qui dare multa potest, multa et amare potest.
seu mare per longum mea cogitet ire puella,
    hanc sequar et fidos una aget aura duos.
unum litus erit sopitis unaque tecto
    arbor et ex una saepe bibemus aqua,

et tabula una duos poterit componere amantis,
prora cubile mihi seu mihi puppis erit.[3]

(2.26.27–34)

True hearts are constant; he who wins by bribing
may have a hundred light loves at his door.
Sail to Cathay, sweetheart, and I shall follow—
we're one, and the same breeze shall fill our sail,
the same shore give us rest, the same tree shade us,
the same spring quench our thirst and never fail.
Who cares how narrow is the bed we lie on,
whether it's at the ship's prow or the stern?

(Carrier's translation)

Housman "corrects" the passage thus:

II xxvi 31 and 32 should be placed before 29: after 28 two verses have been lost: the passage ran thus:

sive iter in terris dominae sit carpere cura
terrestrem carpet me comitante viam;
unum litus erit *positus torus* unaque tecto
arbor, et ex una saepe bibemus aqua.
seu mare per longum eqs.

(*Papers* 33, Housman's italics showing his conjectures),

or if there should be a care for the mistress to take a path on lands she will take a land road with me accompanying; one shore will be a laid bed and one tree for a roof, and from one water we shall drink. Or if the long sea . . .

(translation mine)

It is easy to see what bothered Housman. As the manuscripts transmit the text, in lines 21–26 the speaker muses on his happy life with Cynthia and on her fidelity. Then suddenly, in line 29, she plans to sail. In lines 31–32 the two are back together but on a shore somewhere, and in lines 33–34 they are back aboard a ship. In response to this confusing set of mental images, Housman would have the speaker suddenly think of a trip by land (the lines lost in his hypothetical lacuna), then sit with Cynthia on shore (ll. 31–32), then consider the trip by sea (ll. 29–30), and finally be with her aboard ship (l. 33 ff.; the ship metaphor continues for the rest of the poem).

The manuscripts provide us with a set of images which conflict with each other logically and chronologically. We see, or rather we experience with the speaker, the passing of his imagination through a confused state, in which he reflects upon several possibilities at once. With little help, the reader is expected to experience the various pictures simultaneously. But Housman reorganizes the passage so that the images fit into a sequence that is both logically and chronologically possible. There is no evidence in the manuscripts, other than *N*'s creation of a new elegy at line 29, for a lacuna or dislocation of lines here; rather the only defense of Housman's text is that the lines seem better in that order. The possibility that Propertius preferred the "scrambled" order is not considered.

The foregoing was not designed to single out for criticism a scholar with superb skills in Latin textual criticism. (Indeed, one of Housman's corrections, the postulation of a lacuna after 1.1.11 [*Papers* 29, 42–44], was confirmed by Skutsch's numerical deciphering of Book I ["Structure"].)[4] Rather I wish to question the validity of Housman's assumptions and by implication the assumptions of most Propertian textual critics. Housman found fault with the text as transmitted because it did not follow the traditional principles of literary theory. This theory, initiated by Aristotle and filtered through Horace to the Renaissance, became canonized as the doctrine of the three unities. To be a good literary work, according to the neoclassicists, the work must exhibit a sequence of events that is continuous in time, place, and action; that is, there must not be unaccounted-for lapses in time, changes of place, or reversals of action. Neoclassical rules became incredibly strict, but most classical, as well as neoclassical, literature exhibits these unities; Propertius' work does not. Often Propertius has passages, without lacunae, in which obviously time has elapsed and sometimes the action has taken a dramatic reversal. In 1.8, often divided by editors, Cynthia is contemplating a trip but suddenly decides to stay. In 2.28 Cynthia is ill but then suddenly recovers. White has studied these and similar poems and argued that they exhibit what he calls "dramatic unity" and so should not be divided into smaller poems ("Dramatic Unity"; "Structure"; "Unity").[5] In addition, Propertius makes frequent changes of addressee, that are particularly disturbing to the dramatic situation and have the effect of destroying the unity of place. Moreover, there are numerous distortions of syntax and difficult transitions of thought. The only consistent element in a Propertian poem is what we might call the "unity of speaker," but even this breaks down in 4.1, where Horos and the speaker of the poem address each other.

The lesson from all this is that Propertius will not yield to the traditional modes of textual analysis. While few scholars since the Renaissance would admit to upholding a strict doctrine of the unities (and of course I am not suggesting that Housman himself did so), still they expect a certain continuity of theme and time in a literary work, which Propertius does not even attempt to achieve. He is the poet of non sequitur, and intentionally so.

Interesting, if not always fruitful, are the theories manufactured by classicists to justify dramatic revisions in the text of Propertius. Lachmann's five-book theory has already been mentioned. In the twentieth century there have been theories that the archetypal manuscript, prior to the production of any extant copies, fell apart and was rebound with the pages in the wrong order. Richmond created one of the true anomalies of classical scholarship with his edition of 1928, which exhibited empty spaces where Richmond believed huge chunks of text had been lost. His "reconstruction" of the text was based on his theory that Propertius wrote not in the chaotic manner surviving in the manuscripts but rather in mathematically balanced quatrains.[6] The quatrain theory survives in the radical revisions of Book II suggested by Damon and Helmbold in their 1952 study, although they speak not of archetypal damage but of intentional and massive interpolation by medieval scribes from florilegia. Yet another theory is that of Boyancé, who explains the chaotic movement in

Propertius to "surcharges de rédaction"; the poet went back to completed poems and added portions that were never adequately adapted to their contexts, and hence many poems do not provide the unity we expect from organic works of art ("Surcharges"). Occasionally the standard suggestion among classicists that a posthumous editor in antiquity confused the corpus in an attempt to improve or repair it also appears.[7] All such theories not only create a new scholarly effort, figuring out what Propertius really wrote, as opposed to what is on the page, but also avoid the insistent task of dealing with the text we have.

What is demanded for Propertius is a new approach that transcends the traditional principles of classical criticism, an approach treating Propertius as "anticlassicist," as La Penna calls him (*L'integrazione* 65) in criticizing the methods of Richmond and Damon-Helmbold. Just such a nonclassicist's approach was offered by Ezra Pound, not in scholarly publications but in a type of "translation" of selected pieces, called the *Homage to Sextus Propertius*. Propertius appealed to Pound for three reasons, two of which have been explored by Sullivan (*Pound*) and need little more than mention here.[8] First, Pound felt a political affinity to Propertius. The *Homage* was written in 1917, and Pound felt political pressures, stemming from the Allied situation in World War I, which he believed analogous to Propertius' situation in the circle of Maecenas. For this we have Pound's own often quoted words: "I may perhaps avoid charges of further mystification and obscurity by saying that it presents certain emotions as vital to men faced with the infinite and ineffable imbecility of the British Empire as they were to Propertius some centuries earlier, when faced with the infinite and ineffable imbecility of the Roman Empire" (*Letters* 231). A second appeal, well interpreted by Sullivan, lay in Propertius' employment of *logopoeia*. Sullivan, after extensive quotation from Pound and Eliot, defines *logopoeia* thus: "I suggest then that *logopoeia* is a refined mode of irony which shows itself in certain delicate linguistic ways, in a sensitivity to how language is used in other contexts, and in a development of these other uses for its own humorous or satiric or poetic aims, to produce an effect directly contrary to their effect in the usual contexts" (*Pound* 67). Pound believed that this feature, so characteristic of modernism, occurs in Propertius but not again to any great extent until Jules Laforgue, the nineteenth-century satirist. And politics and style are related in Propertius; this *logopoeia*, as Sullivan argues, is found especially in Propertius' political poems, his *recusationes* (refusals) to write epic poems or praises of Augustus' new programs.

But there is a more important, or at least a more general, reason for Pound's attraction to Propertius. The latter wrote poetry marked by other traits that we now call modernist. The exploration of two of these traits, the interior monologue, a standard feature of the stream-of-consciousness novel, and the imagist or vorticist style, is the subject of the next three chapters. We shall see that a few scholars have applied to Propertius methods like Pound's, although these methods have not become mainstream. The most recent books on Propertius, especially those in English and to a large extent even Sullivan's *Propertius*, do not emphasize them.

If, then, Propertius' poems are not logical structures bound by unity of time, place, and action, what are they? The question, What is an elegy?, opens some of the most fundamental and controversial issues in Latin literature. In the nineteenth century it was customary to answer the question in terms of origins. Scholars searched for examples of Greek elegy resembling the Roman subjective and erotic genre. Since Day's demonstration that no such subjective and erotic Greek genre existed, few have looked, and it is now clear that Roman elegy is a blending of many genres written in Greek and Latin, including Greek elegy, Greek and Roman comedy, bucolic, and even epic.[9] While the same themes run through all of the Roman elegists, namely those singled out for elaboration by Catullus, elegy was certainly not limited to the themes of love and death, and in fact Propertius shows a tremendous thematic variety. Virtually the only distinctive element is the meter, the elegiac couplet. The only other genre using this meter, epigram, featured primarily shorter, wittier, and more caustic poems, and no one confused the two genres; epigrams generally end with a witty turn of phrase (Luck 163).

There is one more constant in elegy, although it has not been generally recognized. A good many of Propertius' poems, especially those with disparate content, exhibit ring-composition. Such a structure has been recognized in the organization of Book I and in the organization of some elegies, but more recently King (*Studies*) has demonstrated verbal ring-composition in nearly every poem in Book I, and Cairns has called attention to the phenomenon as characteristic of Tibullus (*Tibullus* 192–213).[10] Cairns speaks of ring-composition "in a major sense" and "in a minor sense," the former being the creation of an A/B/C/B/A type pattern, the latter being simply the repetition of themes or words in the beginning and end of an elegy. As in Tibullus, both types of ring-composition appear in Propertius.

This structural mode was originally an epic technique, where its primary use was to work digressions into an epic narration.[11] If the narrative is at point A and progresses through B and C to D, the only way to return to A and resume the narrative is through C and B. Let us assume, for example, that the epic poet has his hero on a ship (A) with a hungry crew. In order to eat (E), the crew must beach their ship (B), hunt (C), and perform the preprandial rituals such as sacrificing and setting the table (D). After eating, the crew must clean their tables and wash dishes (D), bury the carcasses (C), launch their ship (B) and resume sailing (A). Homer's use of the technique is far more sophisticated than this, and Bassett has shown that the ancient critics knew of Homeric ring-composition, but one can see the obvious origin of the form; in oral composition or "illiterature" (as Albert Lord's students at Harvard refer to it), the oral poet can expand his material in this way as much as his audience's appreciation (or patience) demands and can omit the digression entirely.

Early Greek lyric and elegy was faced with a problem. Epic works, as Aristotle points out, are unified by narrative completeness, the telling of a complete and significant action. As elegy and the smaller poetic forms evolved out of epic, the question was how to give unity to a non-narrative poem. The use of what Cairns calls "ring-composition in a minor sense" appears as early as Semonides and Alcaeus as a way of providing this unity (Lesky 115, 136). Cairns documents the extensive use of elaborate ring-composition in the Hellenistic period, particularly in Theocritus (*Tibullus* 193). With Catullus 68, sometimes said to be an elegy because of the meter and the appearance there of the themes later to appear in the elegists, ring-composition with elaborate balance comes to Roman literature (although scholars have disagreed on the exact makeup of the ring).[12] At this point ring-composition became a standard part of the elegiac machinery.

Although Propertius' use of ring-composition has been observed, the extent of its use has been far underestimated. However, an appreciation of this use would stabilize the textual criticism of Propertius. An examination of the first five poems in Book II is instructive. Poem 2.1 has been divided by editors and lacunae shown; 2.2 has been joined to 2.3, most recently by Richardson; 2.3 has been divided, most recently by Butler-Barber, and lines 45–54 have been added to 2.4, most recently by Rothstein; in his Teubner edition of 1979, Hanslik shows the end of 2.3 and the beginning of 2.4 as lost. Even the manuscript tradition has difficulties with 2.4 and 2.5, which have been joined together. Ring-composition in 2.6 will be observed in chapter 2.

Kühn has already noticed ring-composition in 2.1, commenting on the echo of "puella facit" (l. 4) with "puella fuit" (l. 78, the last line of the poem; 98). Poem 2.2 has been most maligned of the group, but it is a poem about Cynthia's beauty (*facies*). Hence it is not surprising to find a repetition of "facies" in the third line of the poem and "faciem" in the next to the last line (Bailey, "Experiments" 18 n. 1; King, "Propertius 2.2" 180). Discussion of 2.3 will be postponed momentarily, since it shows what Cairns would call "ring-composition in a major sense," an elaborate ring with mathematical correspondence between the rings. Poem 2.4 does not exhibit ring-composition and may have suffered some textual disturbance (in it Barber prints one of his very few transpositions), but it cannot be a part of 2.3 or 2.5, the unity of which are guaranteed by ring-composition. The ring in 2.5 is created by the vocatives "Cynthia" in the first and last lines of the poem.

The structure of 2.3 is worth consideration in full, both since the poem has undergone so much textual surgery and because the structure, when perceived, is so obvious that unity cannot be in doubt:

'Qui nullam tibi dicebas iam posse nocere,
    haesisti, cecidit spiritus ille tuus!
uix unum potes, infelix, requiescere mensem,
    et turpis de te iam liber alter erit.'
quaerebam, sicca si posset piscis harena
    nec solitus ponto uiuere toruus aper;
aut ego si possem studiis uigilare seueris:
    differtur, numquam tollitur ullus amor.

nec me tam facies, quamuis sit candida, cepit
    (lilia non domina sint magis alba mea,
ut Maeotica nix minio si certet Hibero,
    utque rosae puro lacte natant folia),
nec de more comae per leuia colla fluentes,
    non oculi, geminae, sidera nostra, faces,
nec si qua Arabio lucet bombyce puella
    (non sum de nihilo blandus amator ego):
quantum quod posito formose saltat Iaccho,
    egit ut euhantis dux Ariadna choros,
et quantum, Aeolio cum temptat carmina plectro,
    par Aganippaeae ludere docta lyrae;
et sua cum antiquae committit scripta Corinnae,
    carmina † quae auiuis † non putat aequa suis.

num tibi nascenti primis, mea uita, diebus
    candidus argutum sternuit omen Amor?
haec tibi contulerunt caelestia munera diui,
    haec tibi ne matrem forte dedisse putes.
non non humani partus sunt talia dona:
    ista decem menses non peperere bona.
gloria Romanis una es tu nata puellis:
    Romana accumbes prima puella Ioui,

nec semper nobiscum humana cubilia uises;
post Helenam haec terris forma secunda redit.

hac ego nunc mirer si flagret nostra iuuentus?
pulchrius hac fuerat, Troia, perire tibi.
olim mirabar, quod tanti ad Pergama belli
Europae atque Asiae causa puella fuit;
nunc, Pari, tu sapiens et tu, Menelae, fuisti,
tu quia poscebas, tu quia lentus eras.
digna quidem facies, pro qua uel obiret Achilles;
uel Priamo belli causa probanda fuit.
si quis uult fama tabulas anteire uetustas,
hic dominam exemplo ponat in arte meam:
siue illam Hesperiis, siue illam ostendet Eois,
uret et Eoos, uret et Hesperios.
his saltem ut tenear iam finibus! aut, mihi si quis
acrior, ut moriar, uenerit alter amor!

ac ueluti primo taurus detractat aratra,
post uenit assueto mollis ad arua iugo,
sic primo iuuenes trepidant in amore feroces,
dehinc domiti post haec aequa et iniqua ferunt.
turpia perpessus uates est uincla Melampus,
cognitus Iphicli surripuisse boues,
quem non lucra, magis Pero formosa coegit,
mox Amythaonia nupta futura domo.

You with your boast that nothing more could hurt you—
you're trapped, your spirit's fallen to the snare.
Now for a month you're sleepless; soon, I warn you,
you'll fill another book with your despair.
I've tried to pass the night in sterner studies—
no use, no use. A fish will drown in air,
a wild boar in the sea. My element
is love; I could not live for long elsewhere.
Yet it was not her loveliness that won me—
although no lily ever grew so white;
her skin is snow just touched with Spain's vermilion,
or on fresh cream a rose leaf lying light—
and not her hair, curling around her shoulders,
nor the two torches of her eyes, as bright

as lodestars, nor the silks she loves to shine in.
I am not caught by any lure so trite.
Not these, but that she dances like a Maenad,
like Ariadne, when the revels close;
that when she sings, or with the harp makes music,
there is no voice, no sound, sweeter than those;
that when she writes, her poetry can challenge
the best that even Corinna could compose.
I think Love sneezed—and what's a better omen?—
when on your day of birth the bright sun rose.
These are all gifts the gods alone have given;
you must not think your mother was the source.
No human parentage could so endow you;
such golden gifts are not in nature's course.
You and you only, born the pride of Romans,
will be of Rome the first to share Jove's bed,
being too fair for gods to leave to mortals—
as fair as Helen was, and Helen's dead.
Why should I wonder that our young men love her?
Troy should have perished for this face instead.
I used to marvel that, for any woman,
cities have fallen, nations warred, men bled.
Paris with his demands, and Menelaus
refusing—now I see that they were wise;
who could do less for beauty? Even Priam
might find war justified by such a prize.
Would you surpass the work of ancient artists?
Paint only her: your fame will reach the skies.
The sight of her would set the East to flaming
and in the West make equal fires rise.
I will not stray from her—should I, Love, stab me
with sharper pain than I have known before.
Like Oxen that refuse the yoke, but, slowly
accustomed to it, settle to their chore,
so young men chafe at first against love's fetters,
but then grow calm, enduring more and more,
evil or good; Melampus was imprisoned,
who stole from Iphiclus his cattle, nor

stole them for gain, but out of love for Pero,
the bride he led through his ancestral door.

(Carrier's translation, her italics)

Scholars have doubted the connection between the parts of this poem and the integrity of the whole work. I have "paragraphed" the poem above into sections, as suggested by Camps, and clear connections can be found between these sections.

The first and last sections, each of eight lines, are similar in tone, as has been noted especially by Williams (*Figures* 99) and by Bailey, who comments on lines 45–64: "They return to the original theme of the elegy, the poet's relapse into love's thraldom, for which Cynthia's attractions are his excuse" (*Propertiana*). But these are not the only connections between the two parts. Similar animal imagery appears in the sections; in lines 5–8, the poet compares himself to a fish, in lines 47–50 to a bull. The first and last four-line sections are also tied together by the repetition of "turpis" (ll. 4, 51—each four lines from the end of the poem) and by the subject matter: Melampus the seer ("uates") is compared to the speaker himself, a poet ("uates") (Williams, *Figures* 99). The ends of the poem are thus intricately connected in an A, A2, . . . A2, A fashion, with each section consisting of four lines.

The "B" parts of the poem (ll. 9–22, 33–46), each fourteen lines long, are also tied together. In the first of these sections a strong contrast evolves between east and west. This is developed first through a color contrast, as "snow near Lake Maeotis" ("Maeotica nix") in Scythia "struggles" ("certet") with "Spanish cinnabar" ("Hiberum minium"), eastern white against western red. Then the eastern luxuries—"Arabian silk" ("Arabius bombyx")—are contrasted with western art—"Aeolian plectrum" ("Aeolium plectrum") and Corinna's poems. These are separated by the reference to Iacchus (Bacchus, or Dionysus) and Ariadne. Bacchus, an easterner, migrated west and married Ariadne on Naxos; he also led a military expedition to India. In the second "B" section, again there is a contrast between east and west, focusing especially on the Trojan War as a contest between the two geographical areas. Helen, like Ariadne (who "married" both the westerner, Theseus, and the easterner, Bacchus), appealed to an easterner, Paris, and a westerner, Menelaus. The speaker asserts that Cynthia also would appeal to men of the eastern and western extremities, if exhibited to them as a model for painting. The section ends with the couplet, lines 45–46, which many have said to be of little relationship to the preceding lines:

> his saltem ut tenear iam finibus! aut, mihi si quis
> acrior, ut moriar, uenerit alter amor!

> At least would that I now might be held by these
> boundaries! Or that I might die, if some other sharper
> love will have come to me!
>
> (translation mine)

But actually "finibus" ("boundaries") here retains its normal geographical meaning. Propertius means that Cynthia's beauty threatens to surpass even the limits of extreme east and west set by Ariadne and Helen and that he is not sure he can live with this.

These "B" sections are separated by a ten-line direct address to Cynthia (ll. 23–32), and hence the poem contains the following units:

A: resignation—"uates," "turpis" (four lines)
animal comparisons (four lines)
B: east/west (fourteen lines)
C: direct address (ten lines)
B: east/west (fourteen lines)
A: resignation—animal comparison (four lines)
"uates," "turpis" (four lines).

Williams (*Figures* 99) does not see all of this elaborate ring but realizes that the part he does see leaves little doubt about the unity of this poem; for that matter, it leaves little doubt about the unity of 2.1, 2.2, 2.4, and 2.5. These five poems have appeared problematic, but the demonstration of their unity, guaranteed by ring-composition, should give us reason to doubt that the text has been mutilated in any of the ways described earlier.

Ring-composition is virtually the only way to tie together a poem which has disparate subject matter, especially in an age like Propertius', which has fewer printing conventions than our own. Within the ring of a Propertian poem, almost anything is possible if the connections are conceivable by the human mind. Cairns observes that Tibullus ignores the logical connections of the material and instead forces the material into the "substitute logic" of the ring (*Tibullus* 196). The next three chapters will explore some of the ways in which Propertius creates his own types of substitute logic. But "ring-composition in a major sense," as exhibited by Propertius 2.3 and by many of the poems studied by Cairns in Tibullus, is far less common in Propertius than in Tibullus. Rather Propertius allows his mind to roam freely, associatively to connect ideas both verbally and visually. In this creation of a substitute logic of a particular kind, Propertius' original contribution can be seen.

2
The Propertian Stream

Perhaps the best way to begin an analysis of Propertius' poetic structure is by seeing what his poems are not; let us look at some poems which illustrate the more common, "classical" conception of poetry. Catullus 85 is one of the best known poems in Latin,[1] and it is not difficult to isolate its meaning, to define its poetic existence:

> Odi et amo. quare id faciam, fortasse requiris?
> nescio, sed fieri sentio et excrucior.
>
> I hate and I love. Perhaps you ask why I do this? I do
> not know, but I feel it happen and I am tortured.
>
> (translation mine)

The poem expresses a set of opposing emotions, which the speaker himself does not understand. He feels hate and love toward the object of passion (Lesbia), and he is hurt by the very existence of the opposing emotions. The poem's meaning, then, as Williams (*Tradition* 509) indicates, lies in a logical paradox, in a relationship of feelings which Catullus cannot really communicate. Catullus has chosen a concise style of expression and reduced his verbal quantity to a minimum, as the most effective way of expressing the paradox. The work is harmonious and satisfying, embodying in capsule form the situation later dwelt upon in a variety of moods and manners by the elegists, and we can locate the poetic activity in the relationship of the poet toward his material. The problem is how that material can best be communicated.

In the case of Ovid, at the end of the elegiac tradition, the poetic situation has changed radically. Scholars before Allen ("Sincerity") once spoke of Catullus as sincere and of Ovid as insincere. But what has changed in Ovid is the position of the author vis-à-vis his poetic activity.

We may take *Amores* 1.5 as a rather uncomplicated illustration:

Aestus erat, mediamque dies exegerat horam;
    adposui medio membra levanda toro.
pars adoperta fuit, pars altera clausa fenestrae,
    quale fere siluae lumen habere solent,
qualia sublucent fugiente crepuscula Phoebo
    aut ubi nox abiit nec tamen orta dies.
illa verecundis lux est praebenda puellis,
    qua timidus latebras speret habere pudor.
ecce, Corinna uenit tunica uelata recincta,
    candida diuidua colla tegente coma,
qualiter in thalamos formosa Sameramis isse
    dicitur et multis Lais amata uiris.
deripui tunicam, nec multum rara nocebat;
    pugnabat tunica sed tamen illa tegi,
quae, cum ita pugnaret tamquam quae uincere nollet,
    uicta est non aegre proditione sua.
ut stetit ante oculos posito velamine nostros,
    in toto nusquam corpore menda fuit:
quos umeros, quales uidi tetigique lacertos!
    forma papillarum quam fuit apta premi!
quam castigato planus sub pectore uenter!
    quantum et quale latus! quam iuuenale femur!
singula quid referam? nil non laudabile uidi,
    et nudam pressi corpus ad usque meum.
cetera quis nescit? lassi requieuimus ambo.
    proueniant medii sic mihi saepe dies.

It was Summer, and the day had completed the middle hour; I placed my limbs, in need of rest, on the middle of the bed. Part of the window was open, the other part closed, creating the kind of light woods usually have, as light twinkles when Phoebus is fleeing,

> or when night has left but nevertheless day has not begun. That light should be offered to chaste girls, where timid shame hopes to have a hiding place. Behold, Corinna comes, veiled by a girded tunic, with parted hair covering her white neck, like beautiful Sameramis is said to have gone into her chambers, and Lais, who was loved by many men. I pulled down the tunic, and not much did the thin garment hurt; but nevertheless she struggled to be covered by the tunic, who, since she was fighting just like one who wished not to conquer, was conquered easily amidst her own surrender. As she stood before my eyes, the covering off, there was not a fault in the whole body: what shoulders, what arms did I see and touch! How suitable to be pressed was the shape of her breasts! How flat a stomach under a well-formed bosom! What size and shape her side! What youthful thigh! Why should I mention particulars? I saw nothing not praiseworthy, and pressed her naked body up close to mine. Who does not know the rest? Exhausted we both rested. I hope the middays often turn out thus for me.
>
> (translation mine)

This amusing and popular poem is not difficult to analyze. Ovid first sets the scene, giving the time, the season, a description of his physical position in bed, and a description of the windows and lighting. All of this establishes a mood and provides a feeling of expectation that something will happen. This expectation is fulfilled with Corinna's appearance. Her description, and the less than complimentary comparisons to Sameramis and the famous courtesan Lais, increase the erotic expectations on the part of the reader. The action follows instantly, as the speaker pulls at her clothing. The struggle that follows (with the added detail that she "did not want to win" the battle over her tunic) increases the expectations further, as does the description of her body, from top to bottom, and the lovers' first embrace in line 23. Then follows the typically Ovidian ending which foils the expectations which have been developed so carefully by Ovid and in fact deflates the entire poem.[2] It takes only two lines to dismantle the structure which has required twenty-four lines to build. The reader is left with the effect of a huge balloon, whose size has been increased with each couplet, suddenly being popped. The reader feels entertained but somewhat cheated.

The poem's meaning lies in this very act of deflation, in the very act of disappointing the reader. In Catullus the focus of the poetic act is on the relationship of the poet toward the emotional dilemma he wishes to convey. In Ovid the focus is on the author's attitude toward his audience. In Catullus one feels that the situation the poet describes is unique and important; Catullus is attempting to make the reader understand this situation. With Ovid one feels, at the end of the poem, nothing unique in the described situation. The poem has a narrative structure, but the narrative is foiled, and the reader may even feel somewhat used. So while all three elements of poem, poet, and reader are of course operative for both poets, Catullus and Ovid are at opposite ends of the rhetorical spectrum, a perception that has caused many to refer to Catullus as sincere and to Ovid as insincere.

Catullus and Ovid have been presented here because they represent a recognizable beginning and end of the elegiac tradition. Catullus is clearly struggling to create what later will become the elegiac machinery of Tibullus and Propertius, and at the other end with Ovid, the machinery is running amuck. Somewhere in between these extremes Propertius can be found and explicated. But the reading of nearly any Propertian poem will make it clear that the reader is involved in a very different rhetorical game, in which the focus is not on the audience, as in Ovid, or on the emotions expressed in the poem, as in Catullus, but on the poet (or speaker) himself. In order to understand this game we need to examine one more poem of Catullus.

Catullus 76 has been considered by many (for example, Bishop) to be an elegy:

Si qua recordanti benefacta priora voluptas
    est homini, cum se cogitat esse pium,
nec sanctam uiolasse fidem, nec foedere nullo
    diuum ad fallendos numine abusum homines,
multa parata manent in longa aetate, Catulle,

ex hoc ingrato gaudia amore tibi.
nam quaecumque homines bene cuiquam aut dicere possunt
aut facere, haec a te dictaque factaque sunt,
omnia quae ingratae perierunt credita menti.
quare cur tete iam amplius excrucies?
quin tu animo offirmas atque istinc te ipse reducis
et dis invitis desinis esse miser?
difficile est longum subito deponere amorem,
difficile esse, uerum hoc qua lubet officias;
una salus haec est, hoc est tibi peruincendum,
hoc facias, siue id non pote siue pote.
o di, si uestrum est misereri, aut si quibus umquam
extremam iam ipsa in morte tulistis opem,
me miserum aspicite et, si uitam puriter egi,
eripite hanc pestem perniciemque mihi,
quae mihi subrepens imos ut torpor in artus
expulit ex omni pectore laetitias.
non iam illud quaero, contra me ut diligat illa,
aut, quod non potis est, esse pudica uelit:
ipse ualere opto et taetrum hunc deponere morbum.
o di, reddite mi hoc pro pietate mea.

If there is any pleasure for a man remembering earlier good deeds, when he thinks that he himself is pious, and has not violated any faith, and not abused in any way divine power of the gods for deceiving men, many joys remain prepared for you in long old age, Catullus, from this ungrateful love. For whatever things men can say or do well for anyone, these things have been said and done by you, all which things have perished, entrusted to an ungrateful mind. Therefore why do you torture yourself now more? Why don't you both strengthen yourself in spirit and restore yourself from that condition, and, while the gods are unwilling, cease to be wretched? It is difficult suddenly to put aside a long-standing love; it is difficult, but do this as it pleases. This is the only safety; this must be accomplished by you; do this, whether you can't or whether you can. O gods, if it is your mark to pity, or if you have ever brought the last help to any man now on the very point of death, look upon wretched me, and, if I have spent my life purely, snatch away from me this disease and disaster, which creeping like sluggishness into

> my innermost joints drives pleasures from my whole breast. Not now do I ask this, that she love me in return, or, what is not possible, that she wish to be faithful: I myself hope to say goodbye and to put aside this bitter illness. O gods, return me this for my piety.
> (translation mine)

This poem, whether or not it be an elegy, is excellently conceived. It expands the paradox of Catullus 85 into fuller expression and indeed clarifies the earlier poem. Catullus, as Copley has shown, is torn by what we would call guilt, since he feels only the physical side of love for Lesbia. "It is not from love itself that Catullus wishes release, but from the sense of wrong, of guilt, of unworthiness that has arisen from the persistence of his physical passion after his spiritual and intellectual affection has been destroyed" (39). But the structure of this poem is worthy of note. Williams comments that "the reader must follow the progress of the poet's thoughts and feelings: each successive change wipes out what has gone before," and even goes so far as to call the poem "stream of consciousness" (*Tradition* 408, 412); Luck has presented a similar phenomenon in Tibullus: "Tibullus may lead us through a long cycle of loosely connected themes (as in 1.1), where successive scenes and images blend into each other and seem to have no logical relation, yet dictate to us what we are to feel and carry us gently from one mood to the next" (82).[3] It is precisely in terms of this problematical movement from idea to idea, in a much more exaggerated form and not so "gently," that the structural problems of Propertius must be considered.

Let us begin with Propertius 2.6, a poem that has received little critical attention but that is a good illustration of the difference between Propertius and his more "classical" fellow poets Catullus and Ovid:

> Non ita complebant Ephyraeae Laidos aedis,
> ad cuius iacuit Graecia tota fores;
> turba Menandreae fuerat nec Thaidos olim
> tanta, in qua populus lusit Erichthonius;
> nec quae deletas potuit componere Thebas,
> Phryne tam multis facta beata viris.

quin etiam falsos fingis tibi saepe propinquos,
oscula nec desunt qui tibi iure ferant.
me iuuenum pictae facies, me nomina laedunt,
me tener in cunis et sine uoce puer;
me laedet, si multa tibi dabit oscula mater,
me soror et cum quae dormit amica simul;
omnia me laedent: timidus sum (ignosce timori)
et miser in tunica suspicor esse uirum.
his olim, ut fama est, uitiis ad proelia uentum est,
his Troiana uides funera principiis;
aspera Centauros eadem dementia iussit
frangere in aduersum pocula Pirithoum.
cur exempla petam Graium? tu criminis auctor,
nutritus duro, Romule, lacte lupae:
tu rapere intactas docuisti impune Sabinas:
per te nunc Romae quidlibet audet Amor.
felix Admeti coniunx et lectus Ulixis,
et quaecumque uiri femina limen amat!
templa Pudicitiae quid opus statuisse puellis,
si cuiuis nuptae quidlibet esse licet?
quae manus obscenas depinxit prima tabellas
et posuit casta turpia uisa domo,
illa puellarum ingenuos corrupit ocellos
nequitiaeque suae noluit esse rudis.
a gemat, in terris ista qui protulit arte
turpia sub tacita condita laetitia!
non istis olim uariabant tecta figuris:
tum paries nullo crimine pictus erat.
sed non immerito! uelauit aranea fanum
et mala desertos occupat herba deos.
quos igitur tibi custodes, quae limina ponam,
quae numquam supra pes inimicus eat?
nam nihil inuitae tristis custodia prodest:
quam peccare pudet, Cynthia, tuta sat est.
nos uxor numquam, numquam seducet amica:
semper amica mihi, semper et uxor eris.

No threshold ever has been thronged like this—
not Lais' in Corinth, where all Greece once bowed;

not that of great Menander's heroine,
Thais, around whom gallants used to crowd;
not even Phryne's, she whose lovers' gifts
could have rebuilt old Thebes and made it new.
And through this doorway pass the ones you say—
and do you lie?—are kissing kin to you.
Jealousy eats me at the sight of them,
their portraits even, even a child in arms,
even your mother and your mother's kiss,
the sister who may sleep beside your charms.
What does not frighten me? I even fear
that so-called sister as a man disguised.
O it was jealousy that fathered war;
out of such evils was Troy's fall devised;
the Centaurs, maddened by Pirithous,
broke the bossed goblets in their passionate rage.
No need to name Greek legends. Romulus,
brute-nursed, bequeathed brute cruelty to our age.
In all our history, from the Sabine rape,
there's nothing love's forbidden here at Rome.
Virtue's forgotten—yet true happiness
is hers alone who loves her husband's home.
You maids who built to Chastity her temples—
once you are brides, no limit to your lust,
corrupted in once-decent homes by lewdness
of picture or of book; told, *Learn you must!*
May he be damned, whose vile sophistications
teach infidelity and mock the true!
Years past, no man would tolerate such foulness
nor wink at such vulgarity, as we do—
we who have left our gods to dust and cobwebs
in grass-grown temples where we go no more.
In such an age, love, how can I protect you
or see that evil does not pass your door?
If you will not be saved, no hand can save you.
O Cynthia, be ashamed of such a life!
Then shall no wife nor mistress steal me from you:
you shall be both my mistress and my wife.

(Carrier's translation, her italics)

No major article has been written on this elegy. The only entry under 2.6 in Harrauer's bibliography is a one-page note, in German and over a century old, which upon inspection actually emends 1.6.24.[4] It is not difficult to see the reason for this neglect: the poem's sections do not appear to follow a logical sequence of thought, and in general the poem appears disorganized. Although the manuscripts agree in ascribing unity to the poem and in the order of lines, many editors have suggested transpositions. Richardson, for example, following Scaliger, places the final couplet in the middle of the next poem (some editors have thought the couplet spurious). But even editors who print the poem complete and without transpositions are less than enthusiastic. Butler-Barber, for example, introduce the poem as follows: "While the whole of this elegy deals with the same theme, sc. the faithlessness of women, the sequence of thought is so far from clear that it is hard to resist the conviction that the text has been mutilated. 1–22 present no serious difficulty. . . . But from that point onwards lacunae have, not without reason, been suspected, and the cumulative effect of a series of abrupt transitions is almost overwhelming" (200). Damon-Helmbold (225–26) quote part of this statement, and believing that Propertius composed in four-line stanzas, conclude that "the last two-thirds of the poem is a pastiche of fragments, some of which look genuine enough but are without any discoverable unity" (227). Boyancé has suggested this as one place where Propertius, in revising his text, added a block of material (ll. 27–34) that did not fit its context very well and was never fully integrated into the poem ("Surcharges"). But it is possible to make some sense of this difficult poem.

To begin with, the poem is dominated by one verbal and conceptual idea: this is the *limen* or threshold of the house where Cynthia lives. The poem begins with a description of the *limina* of three famous courtesans Lais, Thais, and Phryne. We are no doubt to imagine these as observed in countless scenes from Greek and Roman comedies (at least this seems to be the effect of the epithet "Menandrean," l. 3) and from the many representations of Phryne in ancient art.[5] These *limina*, the speaker asserts, had smaller crowds than Cynthia's. The poet returns to the idea in the center of the poem: Alcestis and Penelope "loved their thresholds," and "happy" ("felix") is "whatever woman loves the threshold of her husband" (ll. 23–24). The poem returns to the idea again at the end: "What thresholds shall I create, over which never a hostile foot might go?" (ll. 36–37).[6] The poet even considers placing guards at her threshold, but such are useless for the woman who is determined to be unfaithful. The idea of the *limen* is of course important in Roman concepts of marriage. The threshold protects the house and the faith of those in it; one should not need a guard, as Propertius points out. And the sad state of Cynthia's threshold is indicative of the sad state of Roman morality, as the state of Lais', Thais', and Phryne's is of the state of Greek morality. The signs and causes of this decline in the morality surrounding the Roman family is the topic of the poem, and the poem is hung upon this framework of the idea of the threshold which appears in the beginning, middle, and end of the poem.

There are other structural ties within the poem, but perhaps the best way to see these and to interpret the work is to progress through the entire poem as a reader might. The opening couplets establish the theme and create a mental picture based on dramatic and artistic scenes, as I have noted. The poet then turns to a different sort of picture, that of the murals which decorated Roman walls. The poet is jealous of the pictures inside the house, which, as Richardson observes, would be of relatives; Propertius suspects that these relatives are actually rivals. Hence at line 7 the reader crosses the threshold and sees the interior of the house. Here the crowd outside is analogous to the people in the wall paintings. But the paintings are not only of relatives but also of mythological scenes, portraying, for example, Paris and Helen and the battle of Lapiths and Centaurs, and hence the poet moves from the theme of male jealousy (ll. 7–14) to the results of male jealousy in mythology.[7] After these mythological exempla, a curious mixture of Greek and Roman stories, exempla appear refuting the absolute necessity of such a result: Alcestis and Penelope kept their *limina* pure. Richardson has noted that this last exemplum fittingly follows upon Propertius' comment on the uselessness of the temples of Pudicitia (ll. 25–26), and the return to the topic of Roman morality has been made possible by the allusion to Romulus (N.B. the "*nunc . . . Romae*" ["now . . . at Rome"], l. 22) (Reitzenstein 217; La Penna, *Properzio* 46). Propertius then returns to the source of this corruption—wall paintings. After this diatribe the speaker shifts from sources to the explanation of the causes: temples have been ignored (ll. 35–36; Boyancé, "Surcharges" 61; Enk; Reitzenstein 218–19). After one final discussion of thresholds, the poem closes with the assertion that Cynthia will always be "girlfriend and wife." This couplet has displeased many but is very appropriate. Propertius, with the concept of *limina* and his talk of guards and the home, has conceived of his relationship in marital terms: he will treat the threshold as Alcestis and Penelope did, even if Cynthia treats it as Lais, Thais, and Phryne did.

There is then a complex train of thought in the poem, but constant echoes tie the poem together. We might illustrate this as follows, with the major connections on the left side and the minor connections on the right:

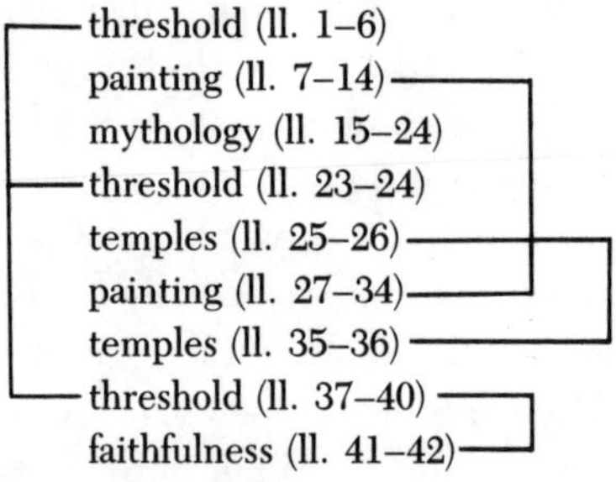

The reader moves from point to point within this structure, and the effect is not at all, as Butler-Barber suggest, "almost overwhelming" (200). There is, furthermore, a lightness in the entire poem. The opening couplets, loaded with Greek names and forms, are a virtual parody of the poet's own mythological catalogs that open poems such as 1.3 (Rothstein; Benediktson, "Catullus" 309–

10). The same effect is achieved by the shift from Cynthia's "uitia" ("faults") in lines 1–6 to the poet's own (jealousy) in the mythological section; this may be to soften the speaker's approach to Cynthia, whom the poet is afraid of offending (Reitzenstein 217; Enk; Rothstein 246). The entire poem is governed by hyperbole, as the poet integrates the conventional theme that social vices, as well as graces, can be traced back into the mythological past, into his own situation. The criticism of Cynthia is real, but the effect of the structure and style of the poem is to divert this criticism by softening it. As often with Propertius, the reader wants to pity the poet yet smile at his mock self-deprecation.

This poem has been examined at length but not because I think it one of Propertius' greatest poems. It is not, although it seems to me better than most critics have believed. Rather I have examined it because it illustrates some important points about Propertius' poetry. It is possible, as we have seen, to move from point to point in Propertius' poem, but the speaker does not make clear to the reader the connections between the segments. There is no internal (or rationally obvious) connection; rather the reader must make these connections alone. The texture of the poem is not governed by the overall structure (which is in fact a static repetition of the concept of *limina*). Rather the poem moves from point to point on a suprarational basis.

This structure is similar to the structures used by certain modernist poets, and especially by Pound, who was an admirer and translator of Propertius. The structure has been called "associative structure," and Sullivan has discussed its appearance in Pound (*Pound* 85, 88–89). Yvor Winters, referred to by Sullivan, describes the associationists' movement: "The associationists provided another principle, however—one of structure: instead of the rational structure of the Renaissance, we were offered a structure based on association" ("Styles" 71). Winters suggests Pound's *Cantos* as an example, and it must be admitted that reading Propertius' poems often approximates the experience of reading the *Cantos*, an experience admirably described by Eva Hesse: "Although these links [in matters of literature and life] may sometimes exist solely in the mind of the poet, or perhaps of the reader, the process involved is essentially one of poetic osmosis. As the curiosity of the reader quickens, the fragments of the poem begin to organize themselves into meaningful patterns" ("Introduction" 13; cf. Robinson 210). In Propertius this "pattern" may be imbedded in the shape of the poem, as in 2.3, or in a series of smaller patterns, as in the next poem to be analyzed; or, as in 2.6, occasionally the poem has no apparent shape (other than ring-composition), and the reader must generate a logical pattern from the dispersed "fragments" (to use Hesse's term). Often a shape is given to the parts of the poem that has little to do with the way the parts are logically related, and there, as I think in Pound, the "pattern" is the meaning generated by the reader, not the physical shape of the poem as transmitted to the reader. In these cases the rational structure is merely a skeleton upon which the flesh and muscle of the poem lean; the important part of Propertius' poem, as we shall see in detail in the next chapters, is the shape and consistency of the muscle and flesh. If Pound is reacting against the "rational structure of the Renaissance," Propertius is reacting against the source from which the Renaissance took its notion of structure—the standard classical conception as illustrated by the poems of Horace, for example, or Vergil.

Another way of expressing this difference between Propertius and the classical poets (or between modernists and neoclassicists) would be to say that Propertius undermines the standard classical distinction between deep structure and surface texture. Meaning, in the standard analysis, consists of a harmonious working of the logical parts of a poem with the diction and figurative language in which the poem is expressed. All of this, of course, goes back to the classical rhetorical distinction, evident everywhere in Cicero, between things (*res*) and words (*uerba*). Thus the standard classical conception of literature is profoundly rhetorical. In Propertius, however, the structure is merely a vehicle of poetic movement, and the majority of the meaning is conveyed by the texture; the reader is left alone to make the logical connections or to generate a deep structure for the poem. In Propertius' mind, it is enough to make a poem if the parts of the poem share in the same situation, feeling, or even mental picture. One is tempted, facetiously, to speak of a "deep texture" and a "surface structure" in Propertius.

It might seem that 2.6 is an unfair example to choose, since the possibility of textual disturbance seems real (although the ring-composition of *limen* would indicate that such disturbance was not on a large scale). But other examples are readily apparent in Propertius of such structural manipulation, that is, of a tension between the deep, rational structure and the surface, associational one. Let us examine 2.25, which has not suffered the same number of transpositions and textual surgeries:

Unica nata meo pulcherrima cura dolori,
    excludit quoniam sors mea saepe 'ueni,'
ista meis fiet notissima forma libellis,
    Calue, tua uenia, pace, Catulle, tua.
miles depositis annosus secubat armis,
    grandaeuique negant ducere aratra boues,
putris et in uacua requiescit nauis harena,
    et uetus in templo bellica parma uacat:
at me ab amore tuo deducet nulla senectus,
    siue ego Tithonus siue ego Nestor ero.
nonne fuit satius duro seruire tyranno
    et gemere in tauro, saeue Perille, tuo?
Gorgonis et satius fuit obdurescere uultu,
    Caucasias etiam si pateremur auis?
sed tamen obsistam. teritur robigine mucro
    ferreus et paruo saepe liquore silex:
at nullo dominae teritur sub crimine amor, qui
    restat et immerita sustinet aure minas.
ultro contemptus rogat, et peccasse fatetur
    laesus, et inuitis ipse redit pedibus.
tu quoque, qui pleno fastus assumis amore,
    credule, nulla diu femina pondus habet.
an quisquam in mediis persoluit uota procellis,
    cum saepe in portu fracta carina natet?
an prius infecto deposcit praemia cursu,

septima quam metam triuerit arte rota?
mendaces ludunt flatus in amore secundi:
si qua uenit sero, magna ruina uenit.
tu tamen interea, quamuis te diligat illa,
in tacito cohibe gaudia clausa sinu.
namque in amore suo semper sua maxima cuique,
nescioquo pacto uerba nocere solent.
quamuis te persaepe uocet, semel ire memento:
inuidiam quod habet, non solet esse diu.
at si saecla forent antiquis grata puellis,
essem ego quod nunc tu: tempore uincor ego.
non tamen ista meos mutabunt saecula mores:
unus quisque sua nouerit ire uia.
at, uos qui officia in multos reuocatis amores,
quantus sic cruciat lumina uestra dolor!
uidistis pleno teneram candore puellam,
uidistis fuscam, ducit uterque color;
uidistis quandam Argiua prodire figura,
uidistis nostras, utraque forma rapit;
illaque plebeio uel sit sandycis amictu:
haec atque illa mali uulneris una uia est.
cum satis una tuis insomnia portet ocellis,
una sat est cuiuis femina multa mala.

Loveliest woman born, and burden of anguish,
for me whose fate forbids the word *Return!*
my books shall leave you famous beyond all others.
(Calvus, Catullus, make this your concern!)
Old soldiers sleep without their rusted weapons;
oxen, grown old, refuse to pull the plough;
the wrecked ship rots on the seashore, and old armor
hangs on the temple walls, unhandled now.
Let me outlive Tithonus, outlive Nestor;
love will not dwindle or be dwarfed by age.
Better to let the great bronze bull of Perillus
burn me, the victim of some tyrant's rage;
better to let Caucasian vultures tear me,
to let the Gorgon stare me into stone.
I will not break, though flint's worn down by water,
and rust takes sword and scabbard for its own.

But no closed door can ever daunt a lover
if he is steadfast and unmoved by threat.
Disdained, he pleads, says his was the wrongdoing,
and seeks the path that wisdom would forget.
You, poor young fool, so proud at love's full tide, now—
learn that a woman's faith is swift and short.
How can the sailor hope to keep a promise
when his sea-shattered vessel limps to port?
how can the prize be claimed by any runner
before the seventh lap around the goal?
The winds of love blow soft; you must not trust them.
Storms may come late, but they will take their toll.
And meanwhile, if she loves you, do no boasting—
keep that joy hidden in your silent heart.
Your own words' echo, once the love is over,
will leave the deepest wound, the sharpest smart.
And though her door is open, enter seldom:
whatever's envied does not long endure.
I'd be as you are now, though, were this era
not one to mock such words as *true* and *pure*.
Corrupted by the age, still I am faithful—
each man must choose the path that he would tread.
But you who argue safety lies in numbers
will come to grief each time you turn your head—
on the one hand, a blond girl to delight you;
a dark one, on the other; both are fair;
here is a Greek, with grace to make you marvel,
and here a Roman, both beyond compare.
Clad in the cheapest clothes or born to the purple,
each is fit means for Cupid and his plan.
Remember the sleepless nights his arrows give you!
One woman is trouble enough for any man.

(Carrier's translation, her italics)

Once again Harrauer lists only textual notes on the poem, and once again critics have been less than enthusiastic. Damon-Helmbold ask, "What, for example, have 39–48 to do with the rest of the poem? We suspect that several lines from 2.18 belong among our *praecepta*" (234). The manuscripts all assert unity for the poem, and there is also internal evidence for this: Richardson (on l. 48) and Rothstein (290) note ring-composition, as the first and final lines echo one another. This echo by itself refutes the assertions of Damon-Helmbold, but in addition, within this outer ring the structure is complex and requires some discussion.

First we should note, as Richardson does, that the poem falls into three parts, "the first addressed to his mistress, the second to the momentarily successful lover, the last to the lover who courts many mistresses" (284). But he does not seem to have noted that within each section there is a detailed structure. The first (ll. 1–20) begins with a brief introduction (the speaker is shut out but will still make his female addressee famous) and then an example appears of what Canter called the "mixed paradigm," where there is a mixture of mythological and historical or natural exempla (223).[8] The speaker begins with two exempla from nature (the soldier and the ship, ll. 5–8). The point in the examples is not clear from lines 1–4, but the lines in themselves are clear: objects and people tend to grow old and obsolete. These exempla from nature and life are followed by two properly mythological ones, which explicitly make the point that the speaker is not subject to the laws of nature (Tithonus and Nestor, ll. 9–10). These thoroughly conventional exempla for old age are followed by an equally conventional exemplum drawn not from nature or mythology but from history (Perillus, ll. 11–12; Renz 61, 55). This exemplum introduces a new idea (implicit, as with the exempla in ll. 5–8) that such obstinacy is painful. This is followed again by two mythological exempla on endurance of suffering (Gorgon and Prometheus, ll. 13–14). The poet closes the catalog the way it began, with a return to natural exempla (the sword and stone, ll. 15–16). Propertius then returns to his own situation (ll. 17–20), using a repetition of "teritur" ("is worn away," ll. 15, 17), so we have a complete ministructure using ring-composition (Propertius, nature/life, mythology, history, mythology, nature/life, Propertius).

It is easy to see what is happening here. The reader is forced through a relatively complex argument, and the elaborate ring-composition keeps the train of thought moving. But the reader must make the logical connections alone; the structure, although itself rational, gives very little help. We might compare what Williams says about Catullus 68 and Vergil, *Georgics* 4.295–358 (both passages with ring-composition): "The myths take the place of statements in primary language and require that the reader's imagination work in co-operation with the poet's to apprehend, rather than reconstruct in discursive prose, the gist of the propositions for which the myths have been substituted" (*Figures* 290). This same type of activity occurs in the second and third parts of the poem. The second (ll. 21–38), linked to the first by "triuerit" ("will have worn away," echoing the "teritur" of ll. 15, 17) moves from address to the rival (ll. 21–22) to nautical allusion (ll. 23–24) to an allusion to chariot racing (ll. 25–26) back to nautical allusion (ll. 27, 28) and to the rival again (ll. 29–38). In the third section a catalog of women (ll. 41–46) is surrounded by couplets which verbally echo one another (ll. 39–40, 47–48: "multos"/"multa," "lumina"/"oculis," "dolor"/"mala" ["many," "eyes," "pain"/"evils"]). Throughout the poem these artificial structures are only a vehicle for the poetic movement. The reader, as was shown in detail for lines 1–20 and as happened also in 2.6, must generate the logical connections. By and large, meaning has been separated from structure. The structure supplies movement, but the reader must generate the meaning from the movement.

One more aspect of 2.25 remains to be considered. There are three different persons or groups of persons addressed in the poem. This is also contrary to the standard classical manner. In most classical poetry the poet addresses one audience throughout a poem; the reader is in the position of eavesdropper upon a piece of communication. In Propertius 2.25 (and this is not atypical of Propertius), the reader overhears several pieces of communication and is pulled from one ostensible audience to another. One result of this is the destruction of the fiction of the communicative act; all three addressees recede into the speaker's mind, and the entire poem functions rather like a soliloquy or even like the semiprivate musings of the persona. We shall see that this effect has been perceived as one of Propertius' means of creating something like the modernists' interior monologue (Lefèvre, "Properziana"; cf. Tränkle 149–50). Here we should observe that the technique adds to the structural effects discussed above; the reader feels that he or she is sharing the private thoughts of the poet instead of witnessing the rational reorganization of these thoughts that most classical poets would have presented.

Propertius 2.25, then, shows significant technical development over the poems previously discussed. Like 2.6, 2.25 consists of musings on a topic (the difficulty and importance of remaining faithful to one woman) but with a much more complex structure. The geometrical structure of 2.3 has become a pattern comprised of three complex rings, each addressed to a different audience (in 2.3 the apostrophe to Cynthia, ll. 23–32, form a separate unit within the ring), and all bound together by echo at beginning and end of the poem. The reader must absorb a great deal of logic and emotion, and while the structure keeps the poem moving, the reader must assimilate alone.

One interesting by-product of Propertius' manner of presentation in a poem is his tendency to move from particular point to particular point, occasionally losing sight of the overall poem. This would be disturbing in Catullus or Ovid but not in a poet who writes as Propertius does. This trait nevertheless often disturbs classicists, who expect Propertius to write in the classical style. An interesting example of this type of poetic movement occurs in 2.28, a poem whose unity is now generally accepted (for example, by White, "Structure"). Margaret Hubbard makes an admirable and extended attempt to defend the entire poem and in the process interprets lines 17–30:

> Io uersa caput primos mugiuerat annos:
> nunc dea, quae Nili flumina uacca bibit.

Ino etiam prima terris aetate uagata est:
hanc miser implorat nauita Leucothoen.
Andromede monstris fuerat deuota marinis:
haec eadem Persei nobilis uxor erat.
Callisto Arcadios errauerat ursa per agros:
haec nocturna suo sidere uela regit.
quod si forte tibi properarint fata quietem,
illa sepulturae fata beata tuae,
narrabis Semelae, quo sit formosa periclo,
credet et illa, suo docta puella malo,
et tibi Maeonias omnis heroidas inter
primus erit nulla non tribuente locus.

Io, by Juno's vengeance made a heifer
drinking Nile water—she is deified.
And Ino, after all her years of wandering,
becomes Leucothoe, the sailors' guide.
Andromeda escaped the grim sea monsters
to find reward as Perseus' faithful wife,
and the Arcadian boar that was Callisto
now as a star saves many a sailor's life.
If the fates mark you for the dark eternal,
the fates of funeral made blest for you—
tell Semele the dangers beauty's heir to;
she whom Jove loved and killed will know them true.
Of all the heroines of Homeric legend,
you, by consent of all, will have first place.

(Carrier's translation)

Hubbard comments that "Jupiter himself is in love with the poet's mistress" (53–54). A number of complications arise with this interpretation, and Hubbard attempts to answer them. Jupiter did not have an affair with Andromeda, so Hubbard argues that lines 21–22 are spurious.[9] Jupiter also did not have an affair with Ino, as Hubbard recognizes, and she suggests some ingenious solutions. But surely two exempla out of five are too many to explain away, and we must seek another solution.

Propertius' stream of thought seems to be this: he is thinking of Hera's jealousy and so alludes to Io, who was an object of the jealousy. This allusion reminds him of Ino, whose name is similar and who also "wandered" and was transformed. We might note the appearance of water in both passages. Ino in turn reminds him of Andromeda (again there is a mention of water). Andromeda, who became a constellation, turns his thought to Callisto, who also became a constellation and who guides sailors (obviously sailing on water; as Ovid tells the story in *Metamorphoses* 2.527–30, Callisto never touches Ocean's waters). Conveniently enough Callisto was an object of jealousy for Juno, and with this link, Propertius is back to the original topic, Hera's jealousy. The latter supplies the connection to Semele, who also conveniently was sister to Io, and puts the poet back in the mainstream of his poem. The poet temporarily leaves his subject and moves through an associative structure that eventually leads back to the point of digression. This is not, strictly speaking, ring-composition, but the use for digression is reminiscent of the original, epic use of ring-composition. The only important thing is that the images are linked in the mind of the poet, and the reader is expected to link them as well.

Perhaps the analysis of one more poem will make clear the points raised here concerning Propertius' use of structure. Propertius 2.34 has been discussed much more than the poems treated above and still is beset by problems of unity and interpretation:

> Cur quisquam faciem dominae iam credat Amori?
>   sic erepta mihi paene puella mea est.
> expertus dico, nemo est in amore fidelis:
>   formosam raro non sibi quisque petit.
> polluit ille deos cognatos, soluit amicos,
>   et bene concordis tristia ad arma uocat.
> hospes in hospitium Menelao uenit adulter:
>   Colchis et ignotum nonne secuta uirum est?
> Lynceu, tune meam potuisti, perfide, curam
>   tangere? nonne tuae tum cecidere manus?
> quid si non constans illa et tam certa fuisset?
>   posses in tanto uiuere flagitio?
> tu mihi uel ferro pectus uel perde ueneno:

a domina tantum te modo tolle mea.
te socium uitae, te corporis esse licebit,
te dominum admitto rebus, amice, meis:
lecto te solum, lecto te deprecor uno:
riualem possum non ego ferre Iouem.
ipse meas solus, quod nil est, aemulor umbras,
stultus, quod stulto saepe timore tremo.
una tamen causa est, qua crimina tanta remitto,
errabant multo quod tua uerba mero.
sed numquam uitae fallet me ruga seuerae:
omnes iam norunt quam sit amare bonum.
Lynceus ipse meus seros insanit amores!
solum te nostros laetor adire deos.
quid tua Socraticis tibi nunc sapientia libris
proderit aut rerum dicere posse uias?
aut quid Erechthei tibi prosunt carmina lecta?
nil iuuat in magno uester amore senex.
tu satius memorem Musis imitere Philetan
et non inflati somnia Callimachi.
nam rursus licet Aetoli referas Acheloi,
fluxerit ut magno fractus amore liquor,
atque etiam ut Phrygio fallax Maeandria campo
errat et ipsa suas decipit unda uias.
qualis et Adrasti fuerit uocalis Arion,
tristis ad Archemori funera uictor equus,
†non Amphiareae prosint tibi fata quadrigae†
aut Capanei magno grata ruina Ioui.
desine et Aeschyleo componere uerba coturno,
desine, et ad mollis membra resolue choros.
incipe iam angusto uersus includere torno,
inque tuos ignis, dure poeta, ueni.
tu non Antimacho, non tutior ibis Homero:
despicit et magnos recta puella deos.
sed non ante graui taurus succumbit aratro,
cornua quam ualidis haeserit in laqueis,
nec tu tam duros per te patieris amores:
trux tamen a nobis ante domandus eris.
harum nulla solet rationem quaerere mundi,
nec cur fraternis Luna laboret equis,

nec si post Stygias aliquid restabit †erumpnas†,
    nec si consulto fulmina missa tonent.
aspice me, cui parua domi fortuna relicta est
    nullus et antiquo Marte triumphus aui,
ut regnem mixtas inter conuiua puellas
    hoc ego, quo tibi nunc eleuor, ingenio!
me iuuet hesternis positum languere corollis,
    quem tetigit iactu certus ad ossa deus;
Actia Vergilium custodis litora Phoebi,
    Caesaris et fortis dicere posse ratis,
qui nunc Aeneae Troiani suscitat arma
    iactaque Lauinis moenia litoribus.
cedite Romani scriptores, cedite Grai!
    nescio quid maius nascitur Iliade.
tu canis umbrosi subter pineta Galaesi
    Thyrsin et attritis Daphnin harundinibus,
utque decem possint corrumpere mala puellas
    missus et impressis haedus ab uberibus.
felix, qui uilis pomis mercaris amores!
    huic licet ingratae Tityrus ipse canat.
felix intactum Corydon qui temptat Alexin
    agricolae domini carpere delicias!
quamuis ille sua lassus requiescat auena,
    laudatur facilis inter Hamadryadas.
tu canis Ascraei ueteris praecepta poetae,
    quo seges in campo, quo uiuet uua iugo.
tale facis carmen docta testudine quale
    Cynthius impositis temperat articulis.
non tamen haec ulli uenient ingrata legenti,
    siue in amore rudis siue peritus erit.
nec minor hic animis, ut sit minor ore, canorus,
    anseris indocto carmine cessit olor.
haec quoque perfecto ludebat Iasone Varro,
    Varro Leucadiae maxima flamma suae;
haec quoque lasciui cantarunt scripta Catulli,
    Lesbia quis ipsa notior est Helena;
haec etiam docti confessa est pagina Calui,
    cum caneret miserae funera Quintiliae.

et modo formosa quam multa Lycoride Gallus
mortuus inferna uulnera lauit aqua!
Cynthia quin etiam uersu laudata Properti—
hos inter si me ponere Fama uolet.

Never entrust to love your lovely mistress.
I trusted mine, and almost she was lost.
Believe me, there's no man but covets beauty,
and none is true. I learned it to my cost.
Love breaks up friendship and can leave kin hostile;
love can turn amity to feud and strife.
Who was it Menelaus welcomed? Paris.
Medea fled her home, a stranger's wife.
Lynceus, could you dare to touch my Cynthia?
Devil! Your hands should have been powerless!
What if she is fickle, unfaithful to me?
Could you have lived and faced your faithlessness?
Kill me—but honestly, with sword or poison—
kill me, so long as you leave her alone.
You may still be my comrade when we're old men;
here, take my fortune, everything I own
except for her; share anything but Cynthia—
I'd not have Jove himself as rival there.
I am so jealous I fear my own shadow;
my own suspicions chill the summer air.
There's only one excuse for you to offer—
say you were drunk. This—this I could forgive.
Don't try to take me in with moralizing;
we learn love's value every year we live.

* * *

Love, after all these years, sends Lynceus reeling.
I'm glad at least that now our gods are his.
What good is Socrates and all that wisdom
that tells us why the world is as it is?
What use are all those old Athenian lyrics?
Your ancient poets are no help in love.
If you must sing, then take, if not Philetas,
Callimachus to make a model of.
Tell what Achelous bore for Deianira—

that river who would rival Hercules;
or how Meander turns and twists through Phrygia,
helpless within its vast complexities;
or how Adrastus' famous horse Arion
spoke at the games for dead Archemorus—
your fate is still that of the Theban Seven,
of Capaneus, of Amphiaraus.
Don't strain your gifts toward Aeschylean verses:
listen to softer rhythms; sway with those.
Shape out your poems on a narrow anvil,
melt your hard heart with your own fiery woes.
Homer, Antimachus—no man moves safely;
beauty will use its power to the full.
The farmer uses goad and yoke and harness
before he plows an acre with the bull.
I'll have to tame your spirit for the hardships
that love requires lovers to endure.
You'll win no girl by showing how the world moves
or how the sun's course keeps the moon secure;
she will not ask who's judge for our hereafter,
or if the lightning's given conscious aim.
Consider me, inheriting no fortune,
bearing no title of ancestral fame:
watch me at banquets; listen to the brilliance
that girls admire—and you make light of this!
Languid, I lie among the fading rose wreaths,
a mark for love his arrows never miss.
Vergil does honor to Apollo's Actium
and to the honors that great Caesar bore;
Vergil can breathe new life into Aeneas,
founding our race on the Lavinian shore—
Vergil, unequalled among Greek or Roman!
Beyond the Iliad's thunder hear it rise,
that other music, telling of the pine woods,
singing the shepherd song that never dies.
With a milk-fed kid, or even a dozen apples,
a country girl, he says, may well be won.
Happy the man who thus can tempt a sweetheart!
Tityrus would praise so virginal a one.

Who would not envy Corydon, loving Alexis,
his master's favorite boy, fresh-cheeked and young?
The wood nymphs prize him, though he drops his reed pipes
in weariness, and leaves his song unsung.
Vergil, like Hesiod you depict the country—
where the wheat grows, and on what hill the vine;
your fingers on the lyre might be Apollo's;
mortal, your music equals the divine.
No man has read your songs who does not love them,
whether he lives as rakehell or recluse.
You are the swan whose least note is pure lyric;
Anser, that poor hack—Anser is a goose.
My themes are all men's. Varro wrote of Jason,
but Varro's love songs—these are what will live;
and passionate Catullus gives to Lesbia
more fame than all the wars of Troy could give;
by love and grief Calvus has kept undying
his dead Quintilia's name; and, dead as well,
Gallus, heartbroken by the cold Lycoris,
still bathes his wounds in the cold streams of hell.

Fate, mark me as you marked these men, that I,
making my Cynthia deathless, shall not die.

(Carrier's translation)

In the case of 2.34 the manuscript evidence for or against unity is ambiguous. All manuscripts except a late (and now not well respected) one join this poem with 2.33. Editors have often divided the poem after line 24. Barber does, although Camps and Enk print it as one elegy. Division has also been suggested after lines 22, 26, and 58; some editors favor division into three poems, and many have attempted transpositions of lines. The only solution seems to be to consider the relationship between the divided portions.

The poem seems to fall into five sections. In the first of these, lines 1–24, Lynceus is chided for his indiscretion. The speaker was foolish to trust Lynceus, since all men search for their own satisfaction, as can be seen in the myths of Paris and Jason (ll. 1–8). By line 15 the speaker refers to Lynceus as "socium uitae" ("partner of life") and "socium corporis" ("partner of body"), a phrase which Bailey finds "perhaps half-humorous" (*Propertiana* 130). He begins to think of himself as paranoid, afraid of his own shadow (l. 19). Why should he be concerned? Lynceus is only an epic/tragic poet, who is incompetent in love.

Lines 25–46 make up the second part of the poem. Here elegy and the tradition of Callimachus and Philetas are contrasted with the epic tradition of Homer and Antimachus (and apparently of Lynceus); epic cannot help in matters of love, and the tragic style of Aeschylus is similarly unhelpful (Vessey 60–62).[10] The details of the passage have resisted coherent interpretation, and the textual corruptions complicate matters, but once again ring-composition is likely. It seems probable that lines 33–36 refer not to epic poems about Hercules, as has been thought, but to poems by Callimachus and Philetas.[11] This is especially plausible if lines 33–34 refer to the amatory and etiological myth of Perimele, which after all explains how the river was "fractus amore" ("broken by love"), although the fragment of Callimachus cited by Reitzenstein seems not to refer to this story about Achelous. Lines 33–36, then, would refer to good material for elegy, lines 37–40 to bad. We have then the following list of points, which fall neatly into a ring:

Socratic poetry (ll. 27–28)
Aeschylean poetry (ll. 29–30)
Callimachean/Philetan poetry (ll. 31–32)
Rivers (ll. 33–36)
Theban Saga (ll. 37–40)
Didactic subject matter (ll.51–52).[12]

The ring is interrupted by the mention of the epic poets Homer and Antimachus in lines 45–56, but these lines fulfill a special function by linking this passage with the Vergilian material in the next section of the poem. This interpretation makes sense with only mild repunctuation of Barber's text (as I have done above) and no further emendation or transposition,[13] and the message of the section is at least apparent: if Lynceus is to be successful in love he must write elegy and accept the "elegiac way of life" (Vessey 63).

Lines 47–58 elaborate on this way of life. The speaker adopts the stance of the *praeceptor amoris* (instructor of love) in this third section of the elegy (Vessey 63–64). Lynceus needs to be "tamed," just like a bull (ll. 47–50). The speaker offers himself as an example, and here one autobiographical and political element enters the poem. Propertius refers to his own unmilitary background (l. 56) and to Augustus' confiscation of lands in 41 B.C., in which he lost property (l. 55). The standard Roman code of ethics is implicitly being contrasted with the speaker's own. What is important to him is his "talent" ("*ingenio*," l. 58) and his power over women, rather than the code of ethics currently being promulgated by Augustus.

In lines 59–80 another comparison is developed; Lynceus' type of poetry has been dismissed, and now Vergilian poetry is compared to elegiac poetry (although we have noted that Antimachus and Homer tie the sections together). The speaker suggests that the *Aeneid* will surpass the *Iliad* (ll. 65–66). In lines 67–80 Vergil's earlier work is discussed. Although perhaps not very accurate in their references, as Camps and Butler-Barber observe, these lines appear complimentary. In lines 75–76 we learn that Corydon was successful in love and hence that Vergil was successful in his version of love poetry, the *Eclogues*. And in lines 77–78 the speaker places Vergil's *Georgics* in the Hesiodic tradition and thus in the tradition of Callimachus and Philetas. The "docta testudo" ("learned lyre") of line 79 must also be interpreted as a compliment to Vergil's learning. The *Eclogues* and *Georgics*, then, are praised in these lines. It is generally believed that the *Aeneid* is also praised, but this seems doubtful (Sullivan, *Propertius* 24–25).[14] The praise of the *Aeneid* is exaggerated; the word "maius" ("bigger" or "greater"), rather than giving a compliment, might suggest to the reader Callimachus' dictum that "a big book is a big evil" (Pfeiffer, fragment 465).[15]

The final section of the poem, lines 81–94, gives a catalog of elegists, Propertius' own genre. The first two couplets contain strong echoes of Vergil's *Eclogues* (Bailey, *Propertiana*; Vessey 67, 75; Camps; Butler-Barber), whose more amatory content provides a smooth transition into the catalog. The list gives the most important Roman elegists and notes that each made his mistress famous. In this respect Catullus surpasses Homer, and Varro Atacinus excells Apollonius Rhodius. The poem ends with the speaker's hope that he and Cynthia may be added to the list.

We are now in a position to assess the unity of the poem. White has argued for dramatic unity in 2.34 ("Unity" 63–68), but more is involved here than drama: the best argument for unity is that the poem has a more complete meaning when all of the parts are considered (Stahl 172–88, 348–54; Lefèvre, "Properce").[16] But we should also note that the end of the poem returns to the beginning, and so the poem once again exhibits ring-composition. The speaker almost lost Cynthia to the poet Lynceus; at the end he reaffirms his fidelity to Cynthia and decides to keep writing elegy instead of epic. There are also verbal repetitions at the beginning and end of the poem. "Formosa" ("beautiful") occurs four lines from the beginning of the poem and four lines from the end. References to Menelaus and Paris occur three lines after the first "formosa," while Helen appears three lines above the second "formosa." Mention of Medea follows closely the reference to Menelaus and Paris, while mention of Jason closely precedes the reference to Helen at the end. So both verbally and thematically a very strong ring is created.

Editors have also suggested that the poem be divided after line 22 or 26, although these are no more persuasive than the usual division. More recently, however, scholars have argued for division after line 58. Damon-Helmbold argue that the tone changes at this point, that Lynceus disappears, and that the last thirty-six lines give a *sphragis* (seal) to the book (238–40); Carter adds that the subject has changed from Lynceus to Vergil and that there is a shift of time, locale, and behavior of Propertius at line 59 (42–43). However, the tone and subject do not change; as I have argued, the comparison between epic and elegy and the political nature of lines 55–59 prepare the reader for the discussion of Vergil's works, and we should note that the shifts at line 59 are considerably milder than those we have seen in 2.25 or than many others in Propertius. Lynceus' disappearance is also typically Propertian. Damon-Helmbold's third argument is persuasive, but in fact the entire poem functions as a "seal" for Book II.

Poem 2.34 has changes of address, emphasis, and emotion, and hence violates what neoclassicists would call the three unities of time, place, and action. But everything is tied together by the ending, which returns the reader to the beginning of the poem, and within the poem are ties between the various units. This structure is close to that of Propertius 2.1, a similar poem in many respects. Boucher compares 2.1, 2.34, and 3.9 to "dialogues" (356), and Camps says of 2.1 and 2.34 that they both show "successive phases of a long and discursive train of thought" (2:2); the poem illustrates what I have characterized as "associative structure," one of Lefèvre's constituent parts of the interior monologue. Each point leads to the next point, and ring-composition bundles the poems together, but as with 2.6 and 2.25, the reader must make his or her own way through the poems and must make the logical connections.

This principle of "free association" is of course the basis of the twentieth-century stream-of-consciousness novel (Humphrey; Bowling; Friedman). The marks of stream of consciousness are, first, that it is concerned with the "*psychological* aspects of character" and, second, that it involves "those levels [of consciousness] that are more inchoate than rational verbalization," that is, the "prespeech level" (Humphrey 1, 4–5; his italics). The most famous aspect of stream of consciousness, the interior monologue, is "the technique used in fiction for representing the psychic content and processes of character, partly or entirely unuttered, just as these processes exist at various levels of conscious control before they are formulated for deliberate speech" (Humphrey 24). The predominant structural mechanism within the interior monologue is, of course, free association.

The applicability of this terminology to the Propertian poems discussed in this chapter should be readily apparent, and indeed the use of interior monologue has been ascribed to Propertius (Lefèvre, "Properziana"; Tartari Chersoni). Lefèvre has presented four traits that create the interior monologue in Propertius: "the alternation of apostrophe," "the fictitious character of the external situation," "the incoherence of the represented time," and "the associative character of the linked material" (28).[17] Humphrey distinguishes the interior monologue from the dramatic monologue and the soliloquy. The dramatic monologue has an ostensible listener present; the soliloquy is addressed to the person actually hearing the text; but in the interior monologue, "no auditor [is] assumed; that is, the character is not speaking to anyone within the functional scene; nor is the character speaking, in effect, to the reader . . ." (25). The overheard monologue is in fact almost unique to Propertius among ancient poets. Most of the poems in Book I are addressed to a specific person (1.1 is an obvious exception), and so qualify, in Humphrey's terms, as dramatic monologues; only a few are addressed to unnamed recipients, and hence might qualify as soliloquies, and only 1.1 has changes of address in the middle (1.3 includes an apostrophe); in Book II, however, less than half of the poems are addressed to one named recipient (most of these to Cynthia), and many poems have multiple changes of addressee (Tränkle 147; Butler-Barber lxiv; Camps 2:1). We have seen such changes in the poems discussed in this chapter and in 2.3, discussed in chapter 1, and we shall see more in the next chapter. At times the speaker, as *praeceptor amoris* (teacher of love), addresses the reader directly and at times addresses Cynthia herself. Poem 2.25 addresses Cynthia, then the reader, and then a generalized plurality of readers. Poem 2.34 is addressed in part to Lynceus, to Vergil, and to the reader directly. The result is a frequent feeling that one is hearing the mental musing of Propertius addressed to no one in particular. This is Propertius' most frequent method of creating interior monologue. Propertius also uses another method of modern stream-of-consciousness authors to develop interior monologue, that is, the disruption of normal linguistic conventions (such as punctuation).

A close analogy to the Propertian method can be found in Dostoevsky's "Krotkaya"—"A Gentle Creature" or "The Meek One" (cf. Friedman 66–69). In the author's preface, Dostoevsky tells us that the following monologue is delivered by a man whose wife has committed suicide, her corpse lying before him on a table. Dostoevsky notes that the man will change addressee, sometimes speaking to himself, sometimes to a kind of jury, and that there will be logical gaps in the presentation. As in Propertius, the effect is to pull the reader into the mind of the speaker. There are also temporal gaps in the narrative. At one point the speaker announces first that he will sleep and then that he has been unable to do so. At another point he reveals that the maid has just entered the room, resigned, and left. This is what the Propertian critic White has called "dramatic unity." At all points, the important thing is not the speaker's thoughts but the movement of thought processes. Here in Dostoevsky, in the early stages of the development of stream-of-consciousness technique, is a method almost indistinct from Propertius'.

Bergson's philosophy contributed a theory of time to stream-of-consciousness thought, but more important for the study of Propertius, it also contributed a theory of perception ("Reality"). Bergson argues for two distinct cognitive operations, which he calls respectively "analysis" and "intuition." In the first operation, we perceive about a thing externally, by examining it from outside; this process is limitless since analysis can be continued indefinitely and hence is never complete. The second operation involves perceiving internally, from the point of view of the perceived; this operation can be completed (by the duplication of the perceived experience). Traditional literature communicates analytical perception; stream of consciousness communicates intuitive perception, since the narration proceeds internally, from the viewpoint of the perceived character. The transmission of analytical perception is the standard western literary mode. One can see it in Greek literature (as for example in the analysis and resynthesis of a worldview in a Greek tragedy), and indeed this is a large part of our intellectual inheritance from the Greeks. One can see the communication of analytical perception in Catullus 85 and Ovid 1.5, discussed at the beginning of this chapter. In each case the poet has analyzed experience and then resynthesized it into a communicable form. But Propertius, like a stream-of-consciousness author, presents experience in a more intuitive form. He does this by avoiding the customary classical presentation of a logical progression of ideas addressed to one recipient and overheard by the reader and instead places the reader directly in the stream of associated ideas and perceptions, thus distorting the passage of time. The experience is transmitted in a form like that in which it might have occurred to the poet (although of course Propertius expends great care in the presentation of this illusion). The poetry of Propertius often strikes a reader as the works of Joyce and similar authors struck Virginia Woolf: "Let us record the atoms as they fall upon the mind in the order in which they fall, let us trace the pattern, however disconnected and incoherent in appearance, which each sight or incident scores upon the consciousness" (Woolf 190). And Propertius is perhaps motivated by the same reaction against classicism as motivated the modernists.

Propertius of course had no access to Freud, William James, Henri Bergson, or any of the other theorists whose ideas underlie the stream-of-consciousness tradition. This tradition represents by and large the post-Lockean reaction to that philosopher's undermining of our perceptual world. But clearly Propertius, whatever labels we should attach, attempts to approximate "psychic processes" and attempts to draw the reader with him through these. It should also be clear that Propertius attempts to transcend the classical or the poetry of the rationally explainable world. Rather he aims at the suprarational, at experience itself rather than at the rational assimilation and presentation of such experience.

At this point only Propertian structure has been considered, and relatively little has been said of the texture of Propertian style. In the next two chapters this texture will be examined, and it will be seen that this texture also aims at the suprarational. Propertius communicates his meaning with what a modernist would call "prespeech" conceptions. The primary vehicles, at least in Propertius' best, most typical poetry, are the image, the metaphor, the nonlogical association.

A word should be said about the sources of these Propertian techniques. Gordon Williams' application of the term "stream of consciousness" to Catullus 76 has been noted; Williams also recognizes that the occasional self-address in Catullus allows the poet to create some special effects. One of these is that "the poet is not taking the world into his confidence; he is merely talking to himself. Form and style blend perfectly." The other is a "dramatic movement of emotion" and "an accompanying interweaving of thematic material" (*Tradition* 412, 464, 466). The same traits are of course those we have described for Propertius in this chapter. It is this perfect blending of form and content, as perceived in the imagination of the poet, the communication of psychological experience, for which Propertius strives. Although Propertius does not use self-address in the manner of Catullus, the former may have developed his own techniques from the Catullan model, and Catullus may have derived his from the Greek sources gathered by Williams. We shall see in chapter 5 that there was a complex of philosophical theories current at Rome in Propertius' time that insisted upon this perfect blending of form and content. But first Propertius' stylistic means of attaining this internal communication must be examined.

3
The Propertian Leitmotif

Propertian poems, as was seen in the previous chapter, can be loose associations gathered about a theme or situation. They are not bound by the standard classical notions of unity or structure, such as continuity of time or action. They can change the addressee or dramatic situation at whim; they can alter the time within which the narrative act occurs; and they can make rapid and frequent alterations of mood or tone. The time, space, and action occur in the minds of poet and reader, something like Bergson's "psychological time," so anything psychologically conceivable is possible in the poems. Yet even to a modernist this stretches the notion of unity. There must be some kind of formal unity other than ring-composition. The interior monologue technique has such a device, what is known as a leitmotif, a recurring refrain throughout a monologue (Friedman 24, 121–38). Propertius also has such a verbal device, or set of verbal devices, as well, and as we might suspect, like Propertian ring-composition, which tends not to penetrate below the verbal into the structural level of the poetry, this device also is not a part of the deep structure but rather lies close to the surface in the verbal texture.

Arnott has explored a device which the ancient comic dramatist Menander used to give unity and continuity to the scenes in his plays (140–46). According to Arnott, Menander repeated at the beginning of scenes words and themes which had been used also at the end of the previous scenes. Considering this a "modern" technique on Menander's part since it occurs also in modern novels, Arnott traces the device also in Greek tragedy and in Callimachus and Theocritus. From the device's occurrence in these latter two, both Hellenistic poets and favorites of the Romans, we would expect to find it in Augustan poetry, and indeed Cairns has observed its use in Tibullus, although he does not elaborate very much, since the main concern there is ring-composition (*Tibullus* 192). In a detailed and thorough study, King has traced the elaborate patterns of verbal repetition in Book I of Propertius and shown that such repetitions are integral parts of the poems in that book and also integral to the structure of the book as a whole ("Studies").[1] In her words, she shows for individual poems in Book I how "word-repetition *consolidates*, *marks transitions*, *bridges* thought-blocks, *unifies*, and *frames* the poem" (40, her italics). There are virtually no structural problems, outside of 1.8, in Book I (if we may make the value judgment of calling them "problems"; actually the "problems" lie with literary critics rather than with the poems), and it is worth observing the technique of verbal repetition in some later, more difficult, and complex Propertian poems, to see what part repetition plays in the stream-of-consciousness techniques described in the previous chapter.

Actually we have already observed one example of the technique in operation. At 2.25.17 Propertius is faced with linking the ring-compositional catalog of lines 5–14 to the mainstream of his poem, and he accomplishes this by repetition of the word "teritur" in lines 15 and 17 ("the sword is worn away . . . but love is worn away by no crime . . ."). A similar verbal technique occurs in 2.34. At line 25 Propertius is faced with linking two parts of the poem which are obviously separated by a time lapse and by a change in the circumstances of the action. Here many authors, including Barber, divide the poem into two poems. Propertius tries to ease the transition through a triple repetition of "amare" ("to love," l. 24, before the temporal gap), "amores" (l. 25), and "amore" (l. 30). But far more sophisticated repetitions can be observed.

Let us begin our examination of Propertian verbal repetition with a poem generally admired and free from the problem of disputed unity. In Propertius 3.6 the speaker addresses the slave Lygdamus (I have italicized the words that will become important in the analysis):

Dic mihi de nostra, quae sentis, *uera puella*;
sic tibi sint dominae, *Lygdame*, *dempta iuga*.
num me laetitia tumefactum fallis inani,
haec referens, quae me credere uelle putas?
omnis enim debet sine *uano* nuntius esse,
maioremque timens *seruus* habere *fidem*.
nunc mihi, si qua tenes, ab origine dicere prima
incipe: suspensis auribus ista *bibam*.

sicin eram incomptis *uidisti*, flere *capillis*?
illius ex *oculis* multa cadebat *aqua*?
nec speculum strato *uidisti*, *Lygdame*, *lecto*?
ornabat niueas nullane gemma *manus*?
ac maestam teneris uestem pendere *lacertis*,
scriniaque ad *lecti* clausa iacere *pedes*?
tristis erat domus, et *tristes* sua pensa ministrae
carpebant, medio nebat et ipsa *loco*,
*umida*que impressa siccabat *lumina* lana,
rettulit et querulo iurgia nostra *sono*?

'Haec te *teste* mihi promissa est, *Lygdame*, merces?
est poenae *seruo* rumpere *teste fidem*.
ille potest nullo miseram me linquere *facto*,
et qualem nolo dicere habere domi!
gaudet me *uacuo* solam tabescere *lecto*;
si placet, insultet, *Lygdame*, *morte mea*.
non me moribus illa, sed herbis improba uicit:
staminea rhombi ducitur ille rota.
illum turgentis ranae portenta rubetae
et lecta exsectis anguibus ossa trahunt,

et strigis inuentae per busta iacentia plumae,
 cinctaque funesto lanea uitta *rogo*.
si non *uana* canunt mea somnia, *Lygdame*, *testor*,
 poena erit ante meos sera sed ampla *pedes*;
putris et in *uacuo* texetur aranea *lecto*:
 noctibus illorum dormiet ipsa Venus.'

quae tibi si *ueris* animis est questa *puella*,
 hac eadem rursus, *Lygdame*, curre uia,
et mea cum multis *lacrimis* mandata reporta,
 iram, non fraudes esse in amore meo,
me quoque consimili impositum torquerier igni:
 iurabo bis sex integer esse dies.
quod mihi si e tanto felix concordia *bello*
 extiterit, per me, *Lygdame*, *liber eris*.

Tell me, Lygdamus, what you think of Cynthia—
speak as a man, and not as Cynthia's slave.
Should I believe you? were they lies to cheer me,
have they been falsehoods, the reports you gave?
The man who brings a message should be honest—
and how much more a slave, who lives in fear!
Tell me again; begin from the beginning—
everything you remember I must hear.
How when she weeps? for you have watched her weeping,
half-hidden by her hair's dishevelled strands.
Was there no mirror on her couch, Lygdamus?
no bright-jewelled rings upon her slender hands?
was it a somber robe that she was wearing?
her rouge, her make-up—were they put away?
was the house sad, the women-servants quiet,
and she among them, knitting the hours away?
and did she use the wool to stanch her weeping
over the words I spoke so bitingly? . . .
"So this is his reward? You heard his promise—
perjury is a crime for slave or free.
How can he leave me so, give me no comfort,
take to his house a woman I would not name?
It gives him pleasure to see me thin and lonely—
if I were dead, he'd mock me still the same!

She's caught him not by love but by black magic!
her witchcraft makes a puppet out of him.
Love philters full of bramble-toads and serpents
she's brewed, and filled the goblet to the brim—
toads, serpents, owls' feathers found in cemeteries.
She's shaped wax images and muttered spells.
Now bear me witness: he'll come crawling to me
and I'll have vengeance. So my dream foretells—
over his empty bed the webs of spiders,
and she false to him even in his embrace."
O if she spoke these words, and spoke them truly,
go back as fast as you can, your path retrace;
tell I send her, with my tears, this message:
Love, prey to anger, keeps its honor still.
A dozen nights I've had no other woman;
my heart no less than hers the same fires fill.
If peace can follow after such a quarrel,
Lygdamus, you'll be free, I swear you will!

(Carrier's translation)

According to Richardson, "the parts of the poem are these: eight verses of introduction (1–8) in which the poet sets his stage pressing Lygdamus to tell the truth, ten verses (9–18) in which he follows Lygdamus' description of the scene at the girl's house and puts questions about details to him, sixteen verses (19–34) of her tirade against her rival, and eight verses of conclusion (35–42) in which the poet sends Lygdamus back with his message of reconciliation" (377). This breakdown is acceptable enough; Camps offers the same schema (3:79). I have spaced the poem above according to these divisions. The issue I would like to consider is how the poet uses repetition to unify the poem and its structural units.

To begin with, the familiar ring-composition is created by the repeated vocatives "Lygdame" ("O Lygdamus") in the opening and closing couplets, in identical metrical position as the first dactylic foot in the second half of the pentameters; the ring is strengthened by the allusions in the opening and closing couplets of the poem to the freedom in store for Lygdamus if all goes well—"dempta iuga" ("yokes removed") and "liber eris" ("you will be free")—(Bailey, "Experiments" 18; Butrica, "Propertius 3.6" 33). These two phrases close the pentameters and follow the vocatives, and hence are juxtaposed. The vocative "Lygdame" appears in this same metrical position in lines 24 and 36, near the beginnings of the third and fourth sections of the poem. The form also appears in lines 11, 19, and 31, at the beginning of the second and third sections, and toward the end of the third. We find it, then, at or near the beginning of each section and near the end of the third and fifth, and hence it runs like a refrain throughout the poem.

These repetitions are reinforced by rhyme: "Lygdame, dempta iuga" (l. 2); "Lygdame, morte mea" ("Lygdamus, my death," l. 24); "Lygdame, curre uia" ("Lygdamus, run on the street," l. 36). "Lygdame, lecto" ("Lygdamus, on the bed") in line 11 is reinforced by the "lecto" of line 23 (a bed is a serious item for an elegist, especially a "uacuo lecto" ["empty bed"], as in both of these lines) and sets off a series of rhyming line endings in between: "loco" ("place," l. 6), "sono" ("sound," l. 18), "facto" ("deed," l. 21) preceding "Lygdame" in line 24, and "rogo" ("funeral pyre") preceding "Lygdame" in line 30. Line 33 again ends with "lecto," line 38 with "meo" ("my"), and line 41, again preceding "Lygdame" in line 42, with "bello" ("war"). "Lecto" then appears near the beginning of the second and fourth sections and at the end of the fourth and helps us follow the center of the poem from "bed" to "funeral pyre," back to "bed," and finally to the "war" from which the poet wishes to be saved. We should also note the reinforcing "lecti" in line 14.

These are the most important repetitions in the poem, but by no means the only ones. The first section ends and the third begins with a reference to the "fidem" ("faith") of a slave; these words ring the second section, as do the nearby words "seruus" (1. 6) and "seruo" ("slave," l. 20). The repetition "teste" ("witness") and "testor" ("I witness") in lines 21 and 31 ring the third section (Bailey, "Experiments" 17, citing Knoche), and "uano"/"uana" ("vain") occurring four lines from the ends of the first and third sections tie them together, as do "uera puella" and "ueris . . . puellis" ("true girl") in lines 1 and 35. Finally crying—"umida . . . lumina" ("wet . . . eyes") and "lacrimis" ("tears") in lines 17 and 37—rings the third section. There are also some repetitions of words and concepts very close to each other, textually speaking: "bibam . . . aqua" ("I shall drink . . . water") in lines 8 and 10 bridging the transition from section one to section two (in the manner described for Menander by Arnott) is the most noteworthy but also apparent are "uidisti . . . uidisti" ("you saw") in lines 9 and 11, "tristis . . . tristes" ("sad") in line 15, and the heavy concentration of references to bodily parts in lines 9–17.

The rather loose structure of the poem, then, is tightened by these internal verbal repetitions. The whole is held together by a verbal ring, and internal rings and links bind to the preceding and succeeding sections. The repetitions also emphasize key words like "*lectum*," "*fides*," "*uerus*," "*uanus*," and so forth. Not many poems in any author will exhibit this much verbal repetition and tightness, but it is well worth examining the poem to see how the poet uses the repetitions to reinforce the structural unity provided by the poem's logical and thematic development.

I may seem to have overdone this. Would a reader hear all of this repetition? Modern readers, to their great loss, tend to read poetry visually. The ancient reader, unable to read silently, would have had a much more aural experience of literature. Stanford, in a thorough discussion of silent reading, shows that "the earliest named silent reader in Europe is, as one might have expected, a man of supreme genius, Julius Caesar" and that "the earliest description of anyone reading a literary work—as distinct from a short message—silently is as late as A.D. 384" (*Sound* 2). Aristophanes was able to ridicule the actor Hegelochus' pronunciation of a line of Euripides (by pronouncing an acute rather than a circumflex accent, he said, "I see a ferret" rather than "I see calm things") three years later (*Ranae* [*Frogs*] 303–4); and Demosthenes, by intentionally placing the accent on the wrong syllable, was able to make an audience shout a word back at him in correction (*De Corona* 98; see Stanford, *Frogs* 99–100). We should not underestimate the aural abilities of a society without mass literacy and the printing press and with less use of writing than ours.

The verbal repetitions in Propertius 3.6 reinforce the underlying logical structure, which would be clear, although much less effective and aesthetically pleasing, without the repetitions. But such repetitions play an even more important role in Propertian poems with less tight structures than that of 3.6. A good illustration is provided by 2.29, which many editors, including Barber, Camps, and Hanslik (in the standard Teubner edition of 1979) have divided into a second poem at line 23 (Richardson prints it as one poem but imports into it parts of 2.2 and 2.30). A conservative text would read something like this (I again italicize words to be discussed and have not, as Carrier has done, separated the poem into two, although I have paragraphed the poem there):

Hesterna, mea lux, cum potus *nocte* uagarer,
nec *me* seruorum duceret ulla manus,
obuia *nescio quot* pueri *mihi* turba minuta
uenerat (hos uetuit *me* numerare timor),
quorum alii faculas, alii retinere sagittas,
pars etiam *uisa est* uincla parare *mihi*.
sed nudi fuerant. quorum lasciuior *unus*,
'Arripite hunc,' inquit, 'iam bene nostis eum.'
hic erat, hunc *mulier* nobis irata locauit.'
dixit, et in collo iam *mihi* nodus erat.
hic alter iubet in medium *propellere*, et alter,
'Intereat, qui nos non *putat* esse deos!
haec te non meritum totas expectat in horas:
at tu *nescio quas* quaeris, inepte, fores.
quae cum Sidoniae nocturna ligamina mitrae
soluerit atque oculos mouerit illa grauis,
afflabunt tibi non *Arabum de gramine odores*,
sed quos ipse suis fecit *Amor* pedibus.
parcite iam, fratres, iam certos spondet *amores*;
et iam ad mandatam *uenimus* ecce *domum*.'
atque ita *mi* iniecto *dixerunt* rursus amictu:
'*I* nunc et *noctes* disce manere *domi*.'

mane erat, et uolui, si *sola* quiesceret illa,
    uisere: at in lecto Cynthia *sola* fuit.
obstipui: non illa *mihi* formosior umquam
    uisa, neque ostrina cum fuit in tunica,
ibat et hinc castae narratum somnia Vestae,
    neu sibi neue *mihi* quae nocitura forent:
talis *uisa mihi* somno dimissa recenti.
    heu quantum per se candida forma ualet!
'Quid tu matutinus,' ait, 'speculator *amicae*?
    me similem uestris moribus esse *putas*?
non ego tam facilis: sat erit *mihi* cognitus *unus*,
    uel tu uel si quis uerior esse potest.
apparent non ulla toro uestigia presso,
    signa uolutantis nec iacuisse duos.
aspice ut in toto *nullus mihi* corpore surgat
    spiritus admisso notus adulterio.'
dixit, *et* opposita *propellens* sauia dextra
    prosilit in laxa nixa pedem solea.
sic ego tam sancti custos deludor *amoris*:
    ex illo felix *nox mihi nulla* fuit.

Last night I wandered drunk along the roadways,
and with no slave to catch me as I fell—
when small boys swarmed around me. I was frightened,
too frightened to count them—why, I cannot tell.
Some carried little torches, some had arrows,
and some had fetters ready for the limb,
and all were naked. One, more arrogant, shouted,
"Now seize him! We have all been warned of him—
he is the one that woman was denouncing"—
and then a rope circled this neck of mine
and my tormentors closed in, with one yelling,
"Death to the man who says we're not divine!
You don't deserve it, but she's waited for you,
while you, you fool, sought for another's door.
Her hair escapes the purple ribbon that binds it,
her eyes, sleep heavy, search for you once more.
She lies in all the fragrance of Arabia,
or in the greater fragrance made by love.

Spare him, now, brothers! he has given his promise;
we'll take him to the house we're guardians of,
and give him over to her safekeeping.
Henceforth stay home when all sane folk are sleeping."

2.29a

At dawn, and wondering who was last night's lover,
I entered—and found her all alone!
alone and never lovelier, even in purple
praying before the Vestals' altar stone,
telling her dreams there to that virgin goddess,
lest any ill luck threaten her or me.
So fair she was, wakening from fresh slumber,
her beauty unadorned for me to see.
"What in the world?" she said. So! You've come spying?
You think my ways untrustworthy as yours?
I'm not so easy. I will take one lover—
you or a new man, if his love endures.
No mark on this bed of another's body,
no sign that two have lain upon this bed.
You do not find me breathing hard or blushing—
you'd know if I'd been false to you," she said.
I would have kissed her, but she held me off, then
jumped up and slipped her sandals on her feet.
I haven't had a happy night since that one,
but that's the fate that spies deserve to meet.

(Carrier's translation)

Some very persuasive arguments for unity in this poem have been presented by White, who well summarizes the arguments of the opposition: line 1 tells of an incident the previous night while the last line seems to refer to an incident several days before, and furthermore the change of address at line 23 is impossible in a unified poem ("Dramatic Unity" 222–25). White shows that lines 1 and 42 can be interpreted in a way not contradictory if, in line 1, "hesterna" ("last") is emended to "extrema" ("extreme," perhaps "late"), or if, in line 42, "ex illo" ("from that") means "on account of that" and not "from that time," and "nulla" ("no") means "not." He also shows that many poems in Propertius have changes of address like the one in line 23 (we have seen several such in this study) and argues that Cynthia's anger in lines 23–42 is caused by the speaker's nocturnal neglect of her in lines 1–22. Finally White considers some arguments for division based on the change of situation in the second part of the poem and argues that there is a time lapse between lines 22 and 23 during which, the audience is to surmise, Propertius slept in the vestibule.

More detailed is the analysis of Cairns, who argues not for dramatic but for generic unity in the poem: both halves are necessary in a komastic poem or paraclausithyron, 2.29 being of the type in which a lover enters the house ("Komoi" 337–49). Cairns finds elaborate ring-composition (A, 11. 1–4; B, 11. 5–14; C, 11. 15–18; D, 11. 19–20; E, 11. 21–22; D, 11. 23–24; C, 11. 25–30; B, 11. 31–38; and A, 11. 39–42) and even suggests that time lapses are typical of komastic poems. The problem of chronology ("hesterna"/"nulla") is solved by rejecting "nox" in line 42, a Renaissance emendation, in favor of the "non" of the manuscripts and interpreting the double negative "non nulla" as an emphatic negative rather than a positive.

These analyses do not answer all of the questions, but they are good interpretations upon which to build. As to verbal and thematic ties between the two parts of the poem, White points only to the "irata" ("angry") in line 9 as matching her behavior in the second part, a point already noted by Enk, and to the references to her beauty in lines 15–18 and 25–30 (once in each part). Cairns notes the balancing "speeches" in each part and the repeated praise in lines 13–20 and 24. Williams, who argues for unity based on "thematic anticipation" in the first part of themes in the second, also finds faithlessness in both parts and "ring-composition by opposites" in the opening and closing couplets and solves the temporal problem by considering lines 1–22 a quotation within the poem as a whole (*Figures* 131–33). But actually there is a much more complex set of verbal ties between the two parts.

Most obvious is the ring, noted by Nethercut, created by "nocte" and "nox" ("night") in the first and last lines of the poem (1828), reinforced by the "me" and "mihi" ("me") in lines 2 and

42. Interestingly the ring is echoed at the center of the poem, lines 21–22, where both "mi" and "noctes" appear again. (Emphasis on pronouns may seem excessive, but King shows very subtle pronominal repetition throughout Book I; here, as occasionally in her analyses, the pronouns indicate the almost selfishly subjective nature of both the speaker's and Cynthia's words ["Studies"].) Forms of *dico* (*say*) appear in lines 10, 21, and 39 relatively near the beginning, middle and end of the poem. This technique of a ring-echo at the center of a poem will be seen again in even more complex form in the next poem to be analyzed. It is also worth noting that in lines 4 and 20, near the beginning and end of the first section of the poem (11. 1–22) and just inside the repetition previously mentioned, is the repetition "uenerat"/"uenimus" ("come"). Moreover there is the repetition "nescio quot"/"nescio quas" ("I know not how many"/"I know not which," 11. 3, 14). Similar to this tie of the beginning of the poem to the middle is the triple repetition "Amor"/"amores"/"amoris" ("love") in lines 18, 19, and 41, which ties the end of the poem to the middle. All of these repetitions reinforce the obvious large-scale structure of the poem: two large units, each comprising approximately half of the poem and each self-contained but bound inextricably to the other unit. And the difficult transition between the two halves, between lines 22 and 23 where there is an obvious breaking of the unities of time, space, and action and where there is a change of address, is eased by the repetitions "I" and "ibat" ("go," 11. 21, 27). Nethercut has remarked on the similarity in sound of "manere"/"mane erat" ("to remain"/"it was morning") in lines 22 and 23, which also eases the transition (although, as Nethercut indicates, this could also be applied as a connection between a pair of elegies).

One word runs like a motif through the entire poem. Both halves of the poem play with the notion of vision; in the first part the poet narrates to Cynthia a vision he had the previous night, and in the second he narrates a morning visit to Cynthia to see if she had slept alone. It is consequently not surprising to see the word "uidere" ("see") and its relatives appear periodically:

"uisa est" (l. 5), "uisere" (l. 24, at the beginning of the second part), and "uisa" (ll. 26–29). Most of these vision words are accompanied by a "mihi" ("to me"), as in lines 6 (although here probably to be taken with "parare" ["to prepare"]), 25, and 29. On a purely verbal level two repetitions in each half are worth noting: "dixit, et" ("he/she spoke, and"), with identical punctuation (or identical sense-pause, as the ancients would have thought of it), appears at the beginning of lines 10 and 39 (Cairns has observed that both halves of the poem contain third-party quotation, to which the words "dixit" refer), and in each case the next line contains the word "propellere" ("to propel"). "Propellere" is not a common enough word that its appearances here, each one line after a formulaic construction like "dixit, et" could be fortuitous. Also probably not fortuitous is the repetition "putat"/"putas" ("think") in lines 12 and 32 and "unus" ("one"), at the end of hexameters and hence rhythmically emphasized, in lines 7 and 33; both pairs, obviously, appear in each half of the poem.

Another tie between the two parts is thematic rather than verbal and depends upon an interpretation suggested by Sullivan. "Nullus . . . spiritus" in lines 37–38 is generally interpreted (as in Carrier's translation, for example) as referring to breathing; Cynthia is showing to the speaker the lack of signs of sexual activity and points to her normal respiration. Sullivan shows convincingly that the reference is to postcoital "bodily odour" and compares the reference to "Arabum de gramine odores" ("odors from herbs of Arabians") or perfume in line 17 ("Propertius 2.29.38" 1–2). Sullivan does not bill his interpretation as an argument for unity, but it certainly must be taken as such in light of the other repetitions explored here.

Rather different but also worth observation is the obvious nonrepetition or antithesis created by "mulier" (l. 9) and "amicae" (l. 31) between the two parts of the poem. The Cupids call Cynthia his "wife"; she refers to herself as his "girlfriend." The antithesis is made more striking by the many verbal and thematic ties. I should add that the elaborate ring Cairns sees is confirmed only by this nonrepetition and by "putat"/"putas," both in the "B" sections, and by "nox" in the "A" and "E" sections. We might conclude, especially since the third "nox" is removed by Cairns, that the ring-composition he suggests is perhaps overly complex.

Finally it is worth examining the closing links in each main section of the poem. Not only are these two sections tied to each other by the repetition "Amor"/"amoris" ("love") in lines 18 and 41 and by the "mi"/"mihi"/"mihi" ("to me") in lines 21, 33, and 42; there is also a set of repetitions within each closing section that gives each half of the poem a sense of closure. At the end of the first section we find "domum"/"domi" ("home") in lines 20 and 22, and in lines 37 and 42, at the close of the second section, "nullus"/"nulla" ("no"), in addition to the "mihi"/"mihi" in lines 33 and 42 already mentioned. One should note here also the repetition of "sola" ("alone") in lines 23 and 24 at the beginning of the second section. These repetitions, then, give a sense of finality to each section of the poem but also the sense of an inextricable bond between the two parts.

This sense of inextricability between the two sections leaves no doubt about the poem's unity. Some might say rather that this is a pair of poems that must be read together and in succession to find full meaning, but this begs the question. To say that two poems must be read together and in succession is the same as to say that they are one poem.

We might now consider the arguments usually presented against unity. Must we adopt Heinsius' emendation of "extrema" for "hesterna" in line 1, or reject "nox" for "non" in line 42 with Cairns, or accept White's interpretation of "ex illo" and "nulla" in line 42? I would offer a countersuggestion which at first glance might seem overly bold: to Propertius such minor problems as chronological or dramatic inconsistencies do not really matter. Would Pound be troubled by such a criticism? As I have insisted, Propertius, like the modernists but unlike the classicists and neoclassicists, is not so narrowly mimetic that he would feel obligated to follow the strict laws of space, time, and human action.

The foregoing analysis shows us how Propertius uses verbal repetition to bind together a two-part poem. But it does not show

how Propertius uses such repetitions in a poem with a meandering, associative structure such as those analyzed in the previous chapter. For such a demonstration Propertius 2.15 is as good an exemplar as any (once more the important words are italicized):

O me felicem! o *nox* mihi candida! et o tu
    lectule deliciis facte beate meis!
quam multa apposita narramus uerba lucerna,
    *quanta*que sublato lumine rixa fuit!
nam modo nudatis mecum est luctata papillis,
    interdum tunica duxit operta moram.
illa meos somno lapsos patefecit *ocellos*
    ore suo et dixit 'Sicine, lente, iaces?'
quam uario amplexu mutamus *bracchia*! *quantum*
    oscula sunt labris nostra morata tuis!
non iuuat in caeco Venerem corrumpere motu:
    si nescis, *oculi* sunt in amore duces.
ipsa Paris *nuda* fertur periisse Lacaena
    cum Menelaeo surgeret e thalamo;
nudus et Endymion Phoebi cepisse sororem
    dicitur et *nudae* concubuisse *deae*.
quod si pertendens animo uestita cubaris,
    scissa ueste meas experiere manus:
quin etiam, si me ulterius prouexerit ira,
    ostendes matri *bracchia* laesa tuae.
necdum inclinatae prohibent te ludere mammae:
    uiderit haec, si quam iam peperisse pudet.
dum nos *fata* sinunt, *oculos* satiemus *amore*;
    nox tibi longa uenit, nec reditura *dies*.
atque utinam haerentis sic nos uincire catena
    uelles, ut numquam soluerit *ulla dies*!
exemplo iunctae tibi sint in *amore* columbae,
    masculus et totum femina coniugium.
errat, qui finem uesani quaerit *amoris*:
    uerus *amor* nullum nouit habere modum.
terra prius falso partu deludit arantis,
    et citius nigros Sol agitabit equos,

fluminaque ad caput incipient reuocare liquores,
aridus et sicco gurgite piscis erit,
quam possim nostros alio transferre dolores:
huius ero uiuus, mortuus huius ero.
quod mihi si secum talis concedere *noctes*
illa uelit, *uitae* longus et annus erit.
si dabit haec multas, fiam immortalis in illis:
nocte una quiuis uel *deus* esse potest.
qualem si cuncti cuperent decurrere uitam
et pressi multo *membra iacere mero*,
nec ferrum crudele neque esset bellica nauis,
nec nostra Actiacum uerteret ossa mare,
nec totiens propriis circum oppugnata triumphis
lassa foret crinis soluere Roma suos.
haec certe merito poterunt laudare minores:
laeserunt nullos *pocula* nostra *deos*.
tu modo, *dum lucet*, fructum ne desere *uitae*!
omnia si dederis oscula, pauca dabis.
ac ueluti folia arentis liquere corollas,
quae passim *calathis* strata natare uides,
sic nobis, qui nunc magnum spiramus amantes,
forsitan includet crastina *fata dies*.

No man more blessed! O night, not dark for me,
beloved bed, scene of such dear delight!
To lie and talk there in the lamp's soft flickering,
and then to learn ourselves by touch, not sight—
to have her hold me with her breasts uncovered,
or, slipping on her tunic, balk my hand;
to have her kiss my eyes awake and murmur,
Why must you sleep? and make her sweet demand.
Shifting our arms, moving to new embraces,
we kissed a thousand kisses multiplied;
then, with the lamp rekindled, fed our senses
on new delights—the eye is love's best guide.
For Paris himself, they say, seeing Helen naked
on Menelaus' bed, loved at first sight;
Endymion, naked, roused the cold Diana,
naked to lie with her throughout the night.

Put on your tunic if you will, my Cynthia;
these furious hands will rip it into shreds.
You'll have bruised arms to show your mother, sweetheart;
when did frustration ever cool hot heads?
Youth's in those light ripe breasts, not yet gone flabby
as women's do when they have borne a child.
O let us love until we are each other—
we on whom Fate these few swift hours has smiled.
It will not be for long. A night will take us
which must refuse to brighten into dawn.
Strain closer to me, lock me in a nearness
that will not fail when time would have it gone.
Remember doves, how they are one in passion,
yoked, as we are, the male and female one?
Love is a frenzy, and it has no limit;
no love, if it is true, is ever done.
Let earth bear winter fruit and shock the farmer,
or let the sun god drive the steeds of night,
rivers run backward, or the seas be shrivelled,
fish dead in unaccustomed air and light—
these things will chance before I love another.
A single year of such nights, should she grant it—
for this I'd give up all three-score-and-ten.
If there were many, I would be immortal;
if there were even one, a god again.
Ah, men are fools who do not pass their life so,
limbs languorous and heavy with much wine.
Did they, there'd be no need for swords and warships,
for sailors' bones to steep in Actium's brine;
no need for Rome to break her heart when Romans
die in the shambles of a civil war.
No god was ever outraged by our wine cups—
men can say this for us, if nothing more.
Do not renounce life while its light is in you.
Given all your kisses, still I'd have too few.
See how the withering wreath lets fall its petals
to float within the cup—O Cynthia, you

and I are lovers blest and hopeful, but
who knows what day may see that last door shut.
(Carrier's translation, her italics)

Many scholars have questioned the continuity of this poem. More recently, however, Rudd and Stahl have provided excellent analyses. Rudd finds four sections to the poem: lines 1–24, 25–40, 41–48, and 49–54. He also finds a coherent theme in each section, reinforced by different imagery in each, and detects grammatical clues that a new section begins at lines 25, 41, and 49, creating a new mood or tone each time. Stahl's division is slightly different: lines 1–10 and 11–24 make up units which he considers "cyclical," and division also occurs at lines 37 and 49.

Rudd's emphasis is on themes and images rather than verbal repetitions, but he does point out a few. "Dum lucet" ("while it is light") in line 49, he notes, echoes the light imagery at the beginning of the poem, thus creating ring-composition. "Nox . . . candida" ("white . . . night") in line 1 and "nox . . . dies" ("night . . . day") in line 24 create an interior ring for the first section, although, as Rudd points out, the meaning has changed, as night becomes equated with death rather than love and day becomes equated with life. Rudd also notes that "fata . . . dies" ("fates . . . day") in lines 23–24 and "fata dies" in line 54 create a tie between the end of the first section and the very end of the poem. Finally, Rudd points out the ties in the references to wine in lines 42, 48, and 52; the first two references "provide a frame for the whole [third] section" (154), and the third reference ties the final section of the poem to the third section, in both of which there is reference to wine.[2] Stahl supports his divisions of lines 1–10 and 11–24 by noting the repetition of lines 3–4 and 9—("quam . . . quanta"/ "quam . . . quantum"; "how . . . how great")—as well as those of "oculi" ("eyes") in lines 12 and 23 and of "nox" ("night") in lines 1 and 24. He also notes that kissing occurs at lines 9–10, 27 (by implication), and 50, that "uita" ("life") is repeated in lines 38, 41, and 49, that there is a thematic tie between lines 10 and 37, and that "nox" is further repeated in lines 37 and 40. Stahl also suggests ring-composition, primarily thematic.

However, these verbal analyses, quite good as far as they go, unfortunately barely scratch the surface. A great many more verbal repetitions appear in the poem, and for the most part they support Rudd's analysis. (It really does not matter whether we accept Rudd's or Stahl's breakdown, since the units could be further divided to satisfy each, but the verbal analysis presented below tends to support Rudd.) The night/day antithesis, for example, runs like a refrain through the poem: "nox" (l. 1), "nox . . . dies" (l. 24), "dies" (l. 26), "noctes" (l. 37), "nocte" (l. 40) and "dies" (l. 54). The night (i.e., love) section of the poem runs from lines 1 to 24, where "nox" is yoked with "dies," and the *dies* (death) section from lines 25 to 54, although the words "dies" in line 24 and "nocte"/"noctes" in lines 37 and 40 interlock the two sections. We have, one might say, a formal accomplishment of the thematic point of the poem: an inextricable interlocking of love and death under the ambiguous symbols of darkness (representing both the act of love and permanent sleep) and day (representing both wakeful life and the "day of death").

The turning point in the poem, structurally, is of course where night becomes day at line 24 or where the theme shifts from love to death. But not only do the "nocte"/"noctes" of lines 37 and 40 interlock the two main sections verbally; there is also a repetition of the word "dies" in lines 24 and 26, on each side of the transition, which eases that shift in tone and theme. Similarly the repetition of forms of "amor" ("love") in lines 23, 29, and 30 ease the transition. Here is our repetition of the type described by Arnott and Cairns, for Menander and Tibullus respectively, in which dramatic scenes or structural blocks of poems are connected by verbal repetition.

More interesting still are the internal rings to the poem (or "frames," as Rudd would call them). In addition to the repetition "nox . . . candida"/"nox . . . dies" in lines 1 and 24, mentioned above, the first section of the poem is characterized by a complex and tight set of repetitions: "nox" (l. 1), "ocellos" ("little eyes," l.

7), "bracchia" ("arms," l. 9), "oculi" ("eyes," l. 12), "nuda" ("nude," l. 13), "nudus" (l. 15), "nudae" (l. 16), "bracchia" (l. 20), "oculos" (l. 23), and "nox" (l. 24). This creates an A/B/C/B/D/D/D/C/B/A pattern, an unmistakable ring centered at the triple repetition of "nudus." This repetition and the ring itself, incidentally, are further tied to the poem by the word "nudatis" in line 5. A second internal ring was noted by Rudd in the third section of the poem (ll. 41–48), where wine references "frame" the passage and also tie it to the fourth section (l. 51). Actually this third section is ringed into the second and fourth sections through the repetitions "uitae"/"uitae" ("life," ll. 38, 49) and "deus"/"deos" ("god," ll. 40, 48). Since the second half of the poem (Rudd's sections 2, 3, 4) is also ringed, as Rudd indicates, by "fata . . . dies"/"fata dies" ("fates . . . day," ll. 23–24, 54), again we find a complex internal ring. When the references to wine are included (ll. 42, 48, 52), the pattern is as follows: "fata . . . dies," "dies," "uitae," "deus," wine, wine, "deos," "uitae," "fata dies," or A/A/B/C/D/D/C/B/A. The center of the ring is the curious diatribe against civil war in lines 43–46. This ring connects the final three sections of the poem, and hence acts, in a complex way, as a repetition of the variety discussed by Arnott and Cairns, in which difficult transitions are bridged by repetitions.

These two internal rings are inextricably linked, however, and the poem does not fragment at line 25. Aside from the interlocking "noctes"/"nocte" of lines 37 and 40, already mentioned, and the recurrent light imagery at the beginning and end of the poem, mentioned by Rudd, there is a repetition of the word "oscula" ("kisses") in lines 10, 50, and, by implication, 26, as noted by Stahl, which helps ring the entire poem. There is also a repetition of "deae" ("goddess," l. 16), which ties with the "deus"/ "deos" in the second part of the poem (ll. 40, 48, in the interior ring described above), and of course, the repetition of "fata" and "dies" at the close of the first and fourth sections, also noted by Rudd, which acts both as an internal ring for the second, third, and fourth sections and as a link between the first and fourth.

There can be no doubt that the radical revisions some scholars have suggested for this poem should be rejected and that the lines as transmitted in the manuscripts are as Propertius wrote them. The structure at the deepest level—the level of argumentative logic, of *res* (things or subject matter) rather than *uerba* (words)—is meandering and even associationist, but an analysis of the textural verbal repetition, which adds a formal aspect, we might even say a structure, to the poem, reveals a literary work as tight, verbally speaking, as Propertius 3.6 or as any poem in Book I. The pattern of the poem is there, offered to the reader by the poet on a purely verbal level, but the pattern has been missed in the zeal to revise the poem into a logical structural pattern such as a more classical, a more rhetorical poet than Propertius might have written.

One of the attempts to revise the poem is worthy of a moment's digression because it offers virtually the only direct conflict between classicists and modernists over Propertius (at least other than in the debate over the worth of Pound's "translations" of Propertius in the *Homage to Sextus Propertius*). In 1935 the classicist Günther Jachmann offered an analysis of Propertius 2.15 entitled "An Elegy of Propertius—A Fate of Transmission," suggesting that a disaster had befallen the text of the poem. A number of transpositions had to be made, and in addition, lines 23–28 and 37–40 had to rejected as spurious. Jachmann believed that the verses, obviously of too poor a quality to be authentic, were doublets for lines 13–16 and 17–22 and were inserted by late classical editors, who would have marked them as spurious, in a kind of early critical edition. These ideas of Jachmann have not become mainstream; in fact Jachmann's name does not appear in the apparatus of Barber or of Hanslik in his 1979 Teubner edition.[3] But the bracketing of the two passages as spurious provoked one of Benedetto Croce's few forays into classical literature.

In an article reprinted in slightly abbreviated form in *Poesia antica e moderna*, Croce criticized the ideas and methods of Jachmann (*Poesia*). While agreeing that the lines in question were not very good, Croce argued for a lack of the kind of late classical edition postulated by Jachmann and showed the circularity of

Jachmann's argument: the state of the text is used as proof of the existence of such an edition, and the existence of such an edition is used to explain the state of the text. Croce suggested that the argument for spuriousness is really an aesthetic judgment rather than a philological one, based on the intuition of the critic rather than on any external evidence of authorship or manuscript transmission. It really does not matter to Croce whether the lines were written by Propertius or not; even if they were, they are unnecessary and disruptive to the poem and hence, even if authentic, should be removed from the text. Croce compares a passage in Carducci which was clearly placed there by the author for certain reasons, but which does not belong to the poem as a work of art; one might compare the argument made elsewhere by Croce, in reviewing Benda's book on Propertius, that in selecting textual variants the editor should choose the "more beautiful" one unless the other is clearly genuine and even then should record personal preference for the conjecture ("Benda" 89).

The argument of Croce implies that much of what classicists do is not worth doing, and it is not surprising that a bitter reply appeared. One can see the same response even today, for example, when a literary critic suggests that the question of authorship or authenticity is not worth asking. The Italian classicist and textual critic Giorgio Pasquali responded to this attack, as he saw it, upon his "friend and colleague." After a statement that could be taken to imply a charge that Croce could not read Greek or Latin, Pasquali suggests that Croce did not understand philology or textual criticism; such editions did exist in antiquity, although admittedly none is extant for Propertius (Croce would do well, Pasquali adds, to read his book on textual criticism). Pasquali suggests that the lines of Carducci are irrelevant, since they are not, unlike the Propertian lines, obviously spurious. The methods of philology, he concludes, are necessary at least to prove the results of intuitive judgments.

I have summarized these arguments in detail because they strike at an issue fundamental to this study. Who was right? In a sense both sides were wrong. The analysis of Propertius 2.15

presented here proves that the lines are not spurious but rather are integral to the text (or, to make a concession to Croce, were considered to be integral by Propertius). Removal of them would truly be a "fate of textual transmission." But in a sense both were right. Analysis of a classical text, as Jachmann and Pasquali believed, must be based on as close a text as possible to what Propertius wrote. But Croce was right that textual criticism is actually also aesthetic criticism and that no degree of learning about scribal errors, about the dating of manuscripts, or even about Greek and Latin style will produce an excellent text for the textual critic who uses that learning to disfigure a classical text. Jachmann's learning is indisputable, but his conclusions are based on an incomplete understanding of the kind of literary work Propertius was attempting to produce. The product may be flawed in the writing (although here I would disagree with Jachmann, Croce, and Pasquali and assert that the poem is quite good), but wholesale corruption of the text in the Middle Ages has demonstrably not occurred. The whole dispute shows how far the classicists had moved from communicating their ideas to a mainstream public and how true were Pound's words used as an epigraph for this book. It is no wonder that Pound's *Homage to Sextus Propertius* was so badly received by classicists when it appeared.

The comparisons of Propertius and Pound in this chapter are not as flippant as they might seem. Pound translated in the *Homage* most or all of the three poems analyzed in this chapter, and there is some evidence that Pound perceived the Propertian techniques described here. Brooke-Rose, in a detailed Jakobsonian analysis of *Canto* 45, has shown that verbal repetition plays a large role in that poem; the *Canto* divides into two halves, which are unified by complex thematic and verbal ties. Most interesting is her comment that "the sounds of the first line function like a statement of motif in music" (61). While clearly there is no proof that Pound took these techniques from Propertius, it is at least worth examining one of the translated texts from the

Homage, VII, to see how Pound managed the Propertian verbal techniques of 2.15:

Me happy, night, night full of brightness;
Oh couch made happy by my long delec-
    tations;
How many words talked out with abundant candles;
Struggles when the lights were taken away;
Now with bared breasts she wrestled against me,
Tunic spread in delay;
And she then opening my eyelids fallen in sleep,
Her lips upon them; and it was her mouth saying:
Sluggard!

In how many varied embraces, our changing arms,
Her kisses, how many, lingering on my lips,
"Turn not Venus into a blinded motion,
    Eyes are the guides of love,
Paris took Helen naked coming from the bed of
    Menelaus,
Endymion's naked body, bright bait for Diana,"
    —such at least is the story.

While our fates twine together, sate we our eyes
    with love;
For long night comes upon you
    and a day when no day returns.
Let the gods lay chains upon us
    so that no day shall unbind them.
Fool who would set a term to love's madness,
For the sun shall drive with black horses,
    earth shall bring wheat from barley,
The flood shall move toward the fountain
    Ere love know moderations,
The fish shall swim in dry streams.
No, now while it may be, let not the fruit of life
    cease.

  Dry wreaths drop their petals,
    their stalks are woven in baskets,

Today we take the great breath of lovers,
  to-morrow fate shuts us in.

Though you give all your kisses
  you give but a few.
Nor can I shift my pains to other,
  Hers will I be dead,
If she confer such nights upon me,
  long is my life, long in years,
If she give me many,
  God am I for the time.

(*Personae* 220–21)

Pound retains the ring-structure technique with the words "night" (ll. 1, 21, 40), "me" (ll. 1, 40, 42), and "long" (ll. 2, 21, 41), which appear in the beginning, center, and end of the poem. There are also interior or concentric rings: "kisses" (ll. 12, 36), "eyes . . . love" (ll. 14, 19–20), and "naked" (ll. 15, 17), which visually shift the emphasis in the poem from the central focus on death (in Propertius) to the nakedness and pleasure of the lovers (in Pound), although in Propertius, as we saw, the triple repetition of "nudus" is in the center of the concentric rings. One might suspect that these verbal effects are really Propertius' verbal repetitions as they survive translation, but this cannot be entirely the case. Pound omits from his translation lines 41–48 and translates the remaining lines in the order 31–34, 49, 51–54, 50, 35–40. Yet in spite of this reorganization of Propertius' text, the complex Propertian ring-composition is retained (or perhaps recreated) by Pound. He cannot have missed entirely the verbal structures described here.

One might justifiably ask at this point where the present chapter has led. What have these verbal repetitions to do with our understanding of Propertius as a stream-of-consciousness writer? Rudd closes his article on Propertius 2.15 with a sagacious comparison of Propertian poetry to music: "As in music, the repetitions are part of the form, and hence part of the meaning. If the result is a beautiful and memorable poem, perfection can be left to look after itself" (155). The repetitions guide the reader through the poems, creating a pattern where the logical structure of the poem offers little or no such pattern. A similar effect is given to the modern stream-of-consciousness novel by the technique called the leitmotif, the repeated word or phrase that offers the reader a handle on the otherwise disoriented material; the leitmotif found its way into literature from music, where it was first employed by Wagner (Friedman 121–38; Cairns, *Tibullus* 193–213). The leitmotif in stream-of-consciousness literature accomplishes many things, one of which, as in Propertius, is the creation of a "substitute structure," as Cairns refers to one of the effects of ring-composition.

A second analogy with the musical leitmotif can be suggested as well. Friedman shows that unlike literature and painting, for example, which are quite different media (literature being temporal, painting spatial, as Lessing emphasizes), literature and music are quite similar. Both are temporal, representing events/notes in temporal succession, and both can be recorded in symbolic shorthand. But, still according to Friedman, there are two differences: literature cannot depict harmony (i.e., two events happening simultaneously as experienced by the reader), and music is circular in time while literature is linear. Modernists have attempted to overcome the first difference through various techniques such as wordplay, but the second can easily be overcome through the leitmotif, through verbal repetition or a kind of refrain. This circularity, so characteristic of music rather than of literature, is also characteristic of Propertius. It explains his preoccupation with ring-composition in the overall structuring of his poems and books and in his patterning of parts of poems (as it also probably explains the dominating preoccupation with ring-composition in modern music [Porter]). And it explains his preoccupation with verbal repetition. In the structureless stream of the Propertian poem, form is created by the ring and the repetition, and these rings and repetitions, whether thematic or purely verbal, are the formal "substitute structures" upon which the poems depend.

4
The Propertian Vortex

In the second chapter I considered Propertius in terms of the interior monologue, a major technique of stream-of-consciousness literature. Another technique, internal analysis, involves the indirect reporting of consciousness by the author; obviously this cannot be accomplished in Roman elegy, since indirect reports are rarely used. But still another technique, sensory impression or the recording by a nearly unconscious consciousness of sensory stimulations, goes to the core of Propertian poetry.

Propertius' style has been frequently discussed, but perhaps the most readable account, in English at least, is in the introduction to Postgate's *Select Elegies*, now more than a century old (lvii–lxxxviii). Postgate did not produce outstanding editions of Propertius; his *Select Elegies*, for example, preserves Lachmann's five-book enumeration, making cross-referencing difficult, and even Housman criticizes his complete edition of Propertius for containing too many transpositions (*Papers* 374–75). But Postgate had an insight into Propertius' poetic temperament. His treatment begins with a discussion of why Propertius' contemporaries preferred Tibullus and concludes, rightly it seems to me, that "his obscurity, his indirectness and his incoherencies were all offenses against the Roman taste" (lviii). This is followed by "the at first paradoxical question, whether he is writing in Latin at all" (lix). Postgate then discusses the various types of obscurity, of which by now the reader should be aware, and gives, as an "explanation of the phenomena," an extremely perceptive account:

> I am sure that my readers will pardon this somewhat long, though imperfect, discussion if I have shewn that in Propertius we are dealing with no ordinary phenomena. These contrasts, these extravagancies, these fluctuations and incoherencies, these half-formed or misshapen thoughts, what do they signify? What is the secret of this chaos? It is that here we are looking on a stage in the realization of thought which is not usually presented to our view. In other writers we see only the full-formed chrystals, sometimes flawed and dim, sometimes bright and clear. In Propertius thought is chrystalizing still. It is still comparatively amorphous and still turbid with development. At such a stage there is hardly limit to possibilities; and almost anything is possible with Propertius. At such a stage the susceptibility to impressions is extreme; and we have seen how potent even the smallest influences are in attracting and deflating Propertius. But I will leave my readers to pursue the metaphor farther for themselves. . . . (lxxii–lxxiii)

I would here like "to pursue the metaphor farther" than Postgate, living in his time, could have imagined.

This last quotation from Postgate should strike some familiar chords by now. The state of the thought in Propertius' poetry, as described by Postgate, corresponds exactly with the prespeech state of consciousness that at the end of the second chapter was asserted as characteristic of the internal monologue. "Chrystalizing," "amorphous" and "turbid with development" are precisely the effects the stream-of-consciousness novelist aims at. "Contrasts," "extravagancies," "fluctuations and incoherencies"—these are the marks of an associative structure, of the free association characteristic of some modernist writing. But most important is the reference to "the susceptibility to impressions." This I would argue is the most important part of Propertius' style. At times the poet borders on what we would call the impressionistic. What is important is not the rational argument being presented, not the dramatic situation or even the emotion the speaker is feeling (these are conventional and, after all, one can read them in any Roman elegist), but rather the dramatic scene itself, and more important, the poet's rather distorted view of that scene and the thoughts that pass through his consciousness as he reacts to and against that scene.

Perhaps the analysis of a poem will make my point more obvious—1.3 is generally regarded as one of his best poems:

> Qualis Thesea iacuit cedente carina
>   languida desertis Cnosia litoribus,
> qualis et accubuit primo Cepheia somno
>   libera iam duris cotibus Andromede,
> nec minus assiduis Edonis fessa choreis
>   qualis in herboso concidit Apidano:
> talis uisa mihi mollem spirare quietem
>   Cynthia non certis nixa caput manibus,
> ebria cum multo traherem uestigia Baccho
>   et quaterent sera nocte facem pueri.
> hanc ego, nondum etiam sensus deperditus omnis,
>   molliter impresso conor adire toro;
> et quamuis duplici correptum ardore iuberent
>   hac Amor hac Liber, durus uterque deus,
> subiecto leuiter positam temptare lacerto
>   osculaque admota sumere et arma manu,
> non tamen ausus eram dominae turbare quietem,
>   expertae metuens iurgia saeuitiae;
> sed sic intentis haerebam fixus occellis,
>   Argus ut ignotis cornibus Inachidos.
> et modo soluebam nostra de fronte corollas
>   ponebamque tuis, Cynthia, temporibus;
> et modo gaudebam lapsos formare capillos;
>   nunc furtiua cauis poma dabam manibus;
> omniaque ingrato largibar munera somno,
>   munera de prono saepe uoluta sinu;
> et quotiens raro duxti suspiria motu,
>   obstipui uano credulus auspicio,
> ne qua tibi insolitos portarent uisa timores,
>   neue quis inuitam cogeret esse suam,

donec diuersas praecurrens luna fenestras,
    luna moraturis sedula luminibus,
compositos leuibus radiis patefecit ocellos.
    sic ait in molli fixa toro cubitum:
'tandem te nostro referens iniuria lecto
    alterius clausis expulit e foribus?
namque ubi longa meae consumpsti tempora noctis,
    languidus exactis, ei mihi, sideribus?
o utinam talis perducas, improbe, noctes,
    me miseram qualis semper habere iubes!
nam modo purpureo fallebam stamine somnum,
    rursus et Orpheae carmine, fessa, lyrae;
interdum leuiter mecum deserta querebar
    externo longas saepe in amore moras,
dum me iucundis lapsam sopor impulit alis.
    illa fuit lacrimis ultima cura meis.'

Like Ariadne lying on the shore
from which the ship of Theseus sailed away,
or like Andromeda, freed from the rock,
who at long last in softer slumber lay,
or like a Maenad, dizzy with the dance,
flinging herself beside the river-bed,
so did my Cynthia seem the soul of rest,
her slender hands beneath her sleeping head.
So did she seem when I came reeling home,
drunk and dishevelled, and the dying light
of the slaves' torches lit the dying night.

Stumbling, I came and stood beside her couch,
drunk, yet not too drunk to be unaware
that love and wine conspired within me now
to drive me to a double madness there.
And so I tried to hold her, rosy-warm
and sleeping, and my toll of kisses take—
quietly, for I know her sudden temper;
I knew how it would rage if she should wake.
Feasting my eyes, I gazed like Argus gazing
on Io's horned head, and smoothed her hair,
and the wreath I had worn laid lightly there.

Apples for your delight: each gift I had
I lavished upon Cynthia whom I love—
placing them stealthily, with hollowed hands,
holding my breath to watch, leaning above,
startled each time you stirred or sighed (although
these were vain terrors) lest your dreaming's course
bring you dark fright, or lest you picture someone—
someone not me—who took your love by force.
But now the moonlight (O officious moon,
trying the window with its lengthened beams!)
wakens her, and with wakening rage she screams,

"Tell me the truth: whose anger, or whose boredom,
has sent you forth from her bed now to mine?
where have you spent the night? whose arms have held you
and left you pale as a ghost and rank with wine?
O may you know the tortures you have taught me;
may you for me that same vain vigil keep—
see my embroidery, see my useless lyre,
how I beguiled the hours I could not sleep.
And while you lay with her, I wept,
till slumber's kind wings touched me and I slept."

(Carrier's translation)

Treatment of details in this poem has varied, but something like a consensus on the form and significance of this poem has been developing.[1] Lyne has shown how the first three couplets develop a clear picture of the Cynthia perceived by the drunken speaker as he enters her room, only to have this beautiful picture disintegrate as Cynthia awakens and demonstrates her true self. Extremely complex verbal repetitions reinforce this disintegration; for example, "languida" ("languid") is repeated (ll. 2, 38), and "purpureum stamen" ("purple thread," l. 41) and "Orphea lyra" ("Orphean lyre," l. 42) refer the reader back to Ariadne and the Bacchant, respectively. Thus the poem exhibits the typically Propertian ring-composition, but here the rings do more than hold together a loose structure; they allow for maximum erosion of the pictorial images.

In fact the poem has three structural aspects, all of which tighten the poetic fabric. First, there is the ring-composition. Second, the poem has a narrative structure. We read about a series of events: the poet's entry, his play with the wreathes and fruit, Cynthia's awakening, and so on. But this narration is a very special type of narration. It is not presented as an objective description of events; rather the reader experiences the events from the viewpoint of the speaker of the poem. Instead of a narrative structure per se, the poem provides a series of visual images; this series of images, within the narrative framework, comprises the third structural aspect of the poem. All three aspects of course work together, and it is this structural coherence of image, logic, and time that has generated such admiration for the poem among classicists.

The imagistic structure referred to here perhaps needs some elaboration. The poem begins, on the narrative level, with the speaker's entry into Cynthia's room where she is sleeping. But the reader does not learn this until line 7; instead, the reader receives three impressionistic mythological scenes, based primarily, as is the subsequent allusion to Io, upon pictorial art, as can be seen from the paintings preserved on the walls at Pompeii (Birt saw as one of Propertius' models the "Vatican Ariadne" shown, for example, in Roscher 1: 1, 545–46); Boucher describes the effect of these images and the one in lines 9–10 as follows: "Thus from image to image the narration of this incident is developed" (55).[2] From the mythological scenes we see the poet, with Cupid and Bacchus on each side, approaching and thinking of making sexual advances. But then an image of Argus and Io appears, to be followed by more action on the part of the speaker. Suddenly the image of Cynthia, built from the earlier images, moves to a new position; her lecture, complete with images of weaving and lyre playing, ends with an image of sleep with wings, again perhaps from pictorial art, as Birt (48–49) and Rothstein suggested, and with tears on her part. But during the poem countless impressionistic and visual elements are added. We are constantly aware of the lighting, for example. The speaker originally sees her in torchlight (l. 10), then in moonlight (ll. 31–34); it is the latter which awakens her. We are given suggestive details as to her sleeping position, an account of her breathing, and most importantly, we are constantly informed of the reaction of the speaker to each image, each impressionistic perception that strikes him. Thus the entire poem occurs within the consciousness of the speaker of the poem. We experience the images and their effects along with him; we have not so much a drama as a drama perceived from the viewpoint of the narrator. This explains the temporal warping in the poem. As in stream-of-consciousness fiction (as inherited from the theory of Bergson), the narrator can adjust the time to reflect his own perception of events. The narrative events correspond not to their actual occurrence in time but to the narrator's perception of them.

The poem then illustrates not a rational argument or a pure narrative, but a succession of images presented from the speaker's viewpoint. These images are in pseudonarrative form, but by and large their relationship is associative rather than internally logical or chronological. And the meaning of the poem is conveyed largely through these associative images. This technique is akin to the modernist imagist or vorticist style chiefly used by Ezra Pound and his associates.

Pound adopted, or so he claims at least, the technique of imagism from Japanese haiku poetry.[3] The Japanese poems consist of a precise visual image that is overlaid by a subsequent (or preceding) narration. Pound's first poems of this type, including the famous "In a Station of the Metro," were written in about 1912 and published in *Lustra* (1915); his own account of the technique is instructive: "The 'one image poem' is a form of superposition, that is to say it is one idea set on top of another" (qtd. in Miner 119). "Superposition" of narrative upon image, in which the image colors the narrative in a surprising manner, is of course the technique of Propertius 1.3, where the jarring disparity between the character and the appearance of Cynthia make the poem's success. It is not surprising that only five years after the haiku discovery Pound published the *Homage to Sextus Propertius*. While Propertius' superposition within the long poem is not as effective as in the Japanese poems, the same may be said of Pound's attempts to incorporate the technique in his longer *Cantos*.

It may be premature at this point to characterize Propertius as an imagist, but it does seem that a consideration of him in these terms will clarify a number of problematical aspects of his style and presentation. One such aspect is his tendency to suggest scenes from pictorial art. This aspect of Propertius has long been recognized (Keyssner; Dilthey; Otto, "Particula Prior" 15–17, "Particula II" 5, 19–21), but more recently Margaret Hubbard (164–66, 173), La Penna (*Properzio*, 103–7), Boucher (41–64), and Papanghelis have pursued Keyssner's attitude that the allusions to art in poetry like Propertius' are really keys to that poet's poetic imagination, rather than a means to discover in Roman literature sources for lost art or lost literature. Roman artists, like Roman writers, did more than copy or translate Greek patterns; they also adapted and revised them. We must examine traditions rather than speculate about specific sources. Propertius in fact uses these traditions, as in 1.3.1–6, with a great deal of sophistication.

This practice is not surprising, and four reasons can be suggested. First, due to the novelty of the scenes at the time, Propertius and his contemporaries must have found them quite striking. Richardson, perhaps the most helpful commentator on this particular topic, comments on 2.6.33–34:

> The introduction of panels with mythological subjects in the decoration of the walls of Roman houses was new in P.'s day. They belong to the late phases of the Second Pompeian Style and are not to be dated before the middle of the first century B.C. At first such pictures were used very sparingly, and the flower of their use is not earlier than the time of Augustus. P. would have been able to see many houses in Rome decorated in the First and severe Second Pompeian Styles (e.g., the Casa dei Grifi on the Palatine) in which there were no figure compositions at all. (229)

These must have been quite impressive. Second, these scenes were especially appropriate for the Roman elegists. As Stenico indicates in discussing the sources of mythology in the murals, scenes from older Greek works are replaced by those of later Greek writers, and amatory material predominates (33–36); the taste of Roman painting resembles that of Hellenistic pastoral, and Propertius found material here easily adaptable to his poetry. Third, Propertius tells the reader in numerous places that he is familiar with Greco-Roman art and that he is strongly affected by it; one of these places, 2.6.9 and 27–30, was examined in chapter 2 (also 1.2.22; 1.14.2; 2.12; 2.31; 3.2.41–44; 3.8.16; 3.9.9–16; 3.21.29–30; cf. Otto, "Particula Prior" 16; Keyssner 264–68, 285). But, most important from our standpoint, Propertius' images tend to be striking, even where pictorial art is not necessarily involved. This has especially been argued by Margaret Hubbard, La Penna, Boucher, and most recently Papanghelis, and it seems questioned only, among modern critics, by Williams, who has maintained that in many passages of Propertius there is "a transformation of ideas which have, or promise to have, a strong visual element into an abstract manipulation of words or concepts" (*Tradition* 423).[4] What Williams seems to have detected is Propertius' unwillingness to complete visual images; the poet stimulates the reader's imagination and then allows the reader to fill in the details. This technique, of stimulating the imagination of the reader by suggesting general types of paintings that he or she has seen, but then allowing the reader to complete his or her own picture, is the essence of Propertius' use of pictorial art. It is also one of the major reasons why I characterize him as an imagist poet.

It is impossible, given the quantity of perished ancient art, to determine exactly the extent of Propertius' use of pictorial art, but I suspect that such use is much greater than has been believed. One example that has escaped notice is in 4.8. In this famous poem Propertius throws a party in Cynthia's absence. Following a highly visual description of Cynthia's departure with her escort, Propertius sets the scene at the party (ll. 27–42):

cum fieret nostro totiens iniuria lecto,
mutato uolui castra mouere toro.
Phyllis Auentinae quaedam est uicina Dianae,
sobria grata parum: cum bibit, omne decet.
altera Tarpeios est inter Teia lucos,
candida, sed potae non satis unus erit.
his ego constitui noctem lenire uocatis
et Venere ignota furta nouare mea.
unus erat tribus in secreta lectulus herba.
quaeris concubitus? inter utramque fui.
Lygdamus ad cyathos, uitrique aestiua supellex
et Methymnaei Graeca saliua meri.
Nile, tuus tibicen erat, crotalistria †phillis†,
haec facilis spargi munda sine arte rosa,
Magnus et ipse suos breuiter concretus in artus
iactabat truncas ad caua buxa manus.

Why should I keep faith with the unfaithful?
she is away. I shall move my camp where I will.
There's Phyllis—she lives on the Aventine, near the temple;
sober, she's dreadful; liquor can lend her charms.
and Teia, in the Tarpeian groves; a beauty,
but one lover's not enough for her drunken arms.
So I called these two to come, lest I should be lonely—
it is always good to learn new ways to woo.
On a secret lawn we spread a couch for our pleasure:
a girl on each side, and I between the two.
Lygdamus served the wine in bowls of chrystal—
summerware; there were tables and dice for bets.
An Egyptian piper played, and we all tossed roses
at pretty Phyllis, clacking the castanets;
Magnus the dwarf hopped to the flute music
on his shrunken stumps of legs like a clumsy ox—
(Carrier's translation)

The reader can easily visualize this scene, as the seating arrangements are clearly described. Propertius reclines between the two courtesans, surrounded by servants and musicians. Scholars, however, have neglected the significance of the musicians. Why are they Egyptian? And what is the reason for the dwarf's inclusion?

It is surely more than to belittle him with the name "Magnus" ("Mr. Big," although some late manuscripts suggest "nanus" ["dwarf"] or "mimus" ["mime"]).

The appearance of the dwarf musician in an Egyptian context would bring to the mind of the ancient reader a famous figure from pictorial art. Magnus represents a *pechys* or dwarf a cubit (*pechys*) in height. Like Magnus, these dwarfs also play musical instruments. They are described by Lucian (*Rhetorum Praeceptor* 6) and by Philostratus the Elder (*Imagines* 1.5). The scene of Father Nile reclining amidst *pecheis* was apparently common in antiquity (Harmon 4:141; Roscher 3: 95–103, 722–23); Fairbanks, in his Loeb edition of Philostratus, refers to the Lucian passage and includes a picture of such a surviving statue in the Vatican Museum (19). Propertius' implied comparison of himself to Father Nile heightens both the humor and the visuality of the passage.

Boucher (63–64) has suggested that the employment of an imagist style, in which images rather than rational argument are the main sources of semantic transfer, also explains Propertius' extended use of mythology. In Ovid's *Amores* mythology is frequently merely a means of attaining rhetorical *copia*, just as his use of pictorial art is less suggestive, or rather less allusive and stimulating to the reader, than Propertius' (Benediktson, "Pictorial Art"); Tibullus is frugal in his use of both techniques (Bright 72–77, 116). Propertius' use of mythology has generated a great deal of scholarship over the past century, and some general theories have been proposed. The most important of these are probably the "symbolic" theory of Allen ("Examples"; "Sunt Qui") and the "idealization" theory of Boyancé ("Properce") and Lieberg ("Mythologie"; cf. Sullivan, *Propertius* 130–34). All of these theories have merit, and they all bear upon the argument made here. But what is important about Propertius' use of mythology is that it allows the poet to transcend the conventional, rational, and orderly means of communication and to transmit ideas to the reader on a suprarational plane. This is clearly the case with his use of pictorial art, and it tends to be the case with mythology as well. One of the standard difficulties with Propertian mythology is that a multiplicity of interpretations accompanies the discussion of any particular passage. The reason for this is not difficult to find. Propertius often lays a logical or dramatic framework for a poem and then offers, by way of elaboration, a myth (or a series of myths) that is suggestive, imagistic, and even impressionistic, but whose relationship to the poem is unclear. One must draw upon one's own ingenuity and background to develop the logical cohesiveness of the poem. And since ingenuities and backgrounds vary, so do interpretations of these passages. This is not to say that Propertius is intentionally vague but rather that his interest lies in the subjective and suggestive qualities of experience and in the manipulation of the subjective experience of his reader. The reader must reassemble that experience in order to read, or rather to experience, the poetry.

Propertius' ability to develop poetic movement with catalogic and pictorial mythology can be seen more clearly in 2.2:

Liber eram et uacuo meditabar uiuere lecto;
at me composita pace fefellit Amor.
cur haec in terris facies humana moratur?
Iuppiter, ignosco pristina furta tua.
fulua coma est longaeque manus, et maxima toto
corpore, et incedit uel Ioue digna soror,
aut cum Dulichias Pallas spatiatur ad aras,
Gorgonis anguiferae pectus aperta comis;
qualis et Ischomache, Lapithae genus, heroine,
Centauris medio grata rapina mero;
†Mercurio satis† fertur Boebeidos undis
uirgineum Brimo composuisse latus.
cedite iam, diuae, quas pastor uiderat olim
Idaeis tunicas ponere uerticibus!
hanc utinam faciem nolit mutare senectus,
etsi Cumaeae saecula uatis agat!

When I was free, I thought to lie alone,
but love, for all our truce, has tricked me still.
Beauty like hers—how can it walk among us?
I cannot blame Jove the insatiable.
Fair-haired she is, her hands are long and slender,

her body's ripe, her step is Juno's own,
or like Minerva's at the island altars,
wearing the breastplate that had made men stone.

She is as lovely as Pirithous' bride
whom at the feast the Centaurs stole away;
lovely as Brimo, when in Thessaly
there by the side of Mercury she lay.
Cynthia can surpass you, goddesses
naked on Ida, whom the shepherd saw!
Though she outlive the Sibyl, may that beauty
be one thing time can neither fade nor flaw.

(Carrier's translation)

The elegy has suffered at the hands of some editors. Richardson, following Scaliger, adds the poem to 2.3 and places lines 9–12 in the middle of 2.29 with the comment that "if the lines are not spurious, they must have strayed here from another poem and been mangled in the process." (Poem 2.3 was examined in chapter 1, 2.29 in chapter 3; there should be no doubt about the unity of either.) Housman (*Papers* 31) wanted to place the lines in 1.3, the excellent poem interpreted earlier in this chapter. Line 11 is certainly corrupt for metrical reasons and hence has been obelized, but the poem makes excellent sense if properly considered.

King has presented a number of useful points about the poem ("Propertius 2.2"). She points out that the poem contains the by now familiar ring-composition, as "hanc faciem" ("this face") in the last couplet echoes the "haec facies" in line 3 (180; previously noted by Bailey, "Experiments" 18, n. 1). She also pinpoints the essential structure of the poem in her analysis of lines 1–4: "The problem of interpretation [whether to accept *ignosco* or *ignoro* in line 4] arises, I believe, because of the view of those who propose that the poem is primarily a retrospective appreciation of the mistress' beauty. Rather, the emphasis is on the thought processes of the lover as he contemplates that beauty in his *uacuo lecto* (1) and decides that he cannot give it up. Thus, his thoughts turn to *furta*" (171). The poem is indeed a flow of "thought processes" rather than a rational argument, and the reader must make his or her way from a considered rejection of love in the first couplet to a resounding reaffirmation in the last couplet: King traces this process from the opening consideration of living alone, to his mistress' "beauty" ("facies," l. 3) and a description of her hair, hands, and walk. This last leads to the exempla of Juno and Minerva, and the latter exemplum leads, via its "violence" and "power," to the exempla of Ischomache and Brimo (the "furta" or "thefts" mentioned in l. 4) and back to the two Olympians via the reference to the "Judgment of Paris," involving the two Olympians already mentioned as well as Venus (Helm, in Pauly 23: 786; Kuinoel, qtd. in Enk 2. 2), and closing with a return to the mistress' "facies." Richardson presents a similar interpretation, even though he combines 2.2 and 2.3, which is worth quotation in full due to its relevance to a stream-of-consciousness view of Propertius: "P. experiments with thought processes, their lack of logical neatness, their failure to maintain a constant point of view, their way of building to rushes of intensity only to relapse into the wayward and aimless. Elsewhere he compares his inspiration to a stream (cf., e.g., 2.4.19–20); here he allows his work to move like a stream" (218).

To King's analysis I would add several points. First, the "thought processes" she illustrates are largely associative. The transferrence of ideas within the exempla is not made clear by rational presentation on the part of the poet. Rather the reader must draw these inferences from clues provided by the poet. Second, the poem's structure is essentially imagist. The reader is presented with a succession of visual images; these images are increasingly pictorial, as more detail is added to each scene and familiar scenes from pictorial art such as the Lapiths and Centaurs (King, "Propertius 2.2" 172) are presented. Only Boucher (56–57, 372–73) has emphasized the pictorial aspects of this poem. Boucher, who even uses the word "superposition," sees lines 9–12 as a "surcharge de rédaction," or overlay of a second, revised draft upon a first, and notes that the exempla of Ischomache and the Judgment of Paris given here, in the latter of which the goddesses are unclothed, are "pictorial variants" (373). He concludes: "It is the visual imagination of the poet which constitutes the interior tie of this development."[5] The reader is progressively absorbed in these exotic scenes and thus is guided through the difficult (because latent rather than patent) rational structure of the poem. The effect is rather the reverse of 1.3. There a clear and stimulating set of images appears at the beginning of the poem and slowly disintegrates before the reader's view; here the effect is increasingly pictorial and engrossing, and the reader is consequently forced to put the images together and to make sense of the poem.

Other series of exempla work this way in Propertius, and the technique illustrated here is by no means atypical of the poet. His mythological catalogs, where a series of brief exempla are presented, push the reader through some difficult logical sequences. This is entirely different from Ovid's *Amores*, where mythological catalogs are primarily a means of generating material and entertaining the audience. A good illustration of this is offered by comparing Tibullus 1.4.61–64 and Ovid, *Amores* 3.12.21–40. Both poets have identical opportunities to illustrate the mythological figures made popular by poets. While Tibullus is content with two exempla (Scylla and Pelops), Ovid names seventeen figures or groups of figures: Scylla (or a blend of both Scyllas), Perseus, Medusa and Pegasus, Cerberus, Enceladus, the Sirens, Aeolus, Tantalus, Niobe, Callisto, Zeus and Leda, Danae and Europa, Proteus, the Spartoi, the Golden Fleece, the Heliades, the ships of Aeneas, Atreus, and Amphion. The Ovidian passage lists figures in no apparent order and without any visible standard of choice (although with carefully devised style; cf. Renz 77–78), even though women, transformations, and the underworld are general themes. The catalog is a barrage of mythological learning, presented in a fashion that demands mythological sophistication on the part of the reader, since many of the figures are alluded to without being named. But this type of catalog is not common in Propertius. Rather Propertius offers catalogs that employ imagist style in order to generate implied rational structures; 1.3 and 2.2 function as such, and other examples could be presented.

The use of such catalogs has a long literary history, and certainly Propertius' uses of the catalogic format are developed, through Hellenistic "Kollektivgedichte" or "catalog poems" (Martini 168–75) and through Catullus 58 B (Benediktson, "Catullus"), from very old literary devices. Just as free association governs the interrelationships in the catalogs and just as the catalogs try to convey images rather than logically to present arguments, events, or concepts, the catalogs analyzed here present ideas in a suprarational sphere. Propertius conveys experience itself, with the appearance at least of duplicating the experience of the poet, rather than a rationally distilled account of that experience.

One of the more fruitful spheres of experience probed by modern stream-of-consciousness writers is people's consciousness during dreams. *Finnegans Wake*, for example, is a tour de force journey into a subconscious dreamworld. Modernists have the symbolist theories of Freud and Jung upon which to draw and Propertius did not, but the ancient poet still found that world an ideal ground for his associative and imagist techniques as in 2.26, in which the speaker narrates a particular dream about Cynthia and then reflects upon his own dream:

Vidi te in somnis fracta, mea uita, carina
    Ionio lassas ducere rore manus,
et quaecumque in me fueras mentita fateri,
    nec iam umore grauis tollere posse comas,
qualem purpureis agitatam fluctibus Hellen,
    aurea quam molli tergore uexit ouis.
quam timui, ne forte tuum mare nomen haberet
    atque tua labens nauita fleret aqua!
quae tum ego Neptuno, quae tum cum Castore fratri,
    quaeque tibi excepi, iam dea, Leucothoe!
at tu uix primas extollens gurgite palmas
    saepe meum nomen iam peritura uocas.

quod si forte tuos uidisset Glaucus ocellos,
esses Ionii facta puella maris,
et tibi ob inuidiam Nereides increpitarent,
candida Nesaee, caerula Cymothoe.
sed tibi subsidio delphinum currere uidi,
qui, puto, Arioniam uexerat ante lyram.
iamque ego conabar summo me mittere saxo,
cum mihi discussit talia uisa metus.
nunc admirentur quod tam mihi pulchra puella
seruiat et tota dicar in urbe potens!
non, si Cambysae redeant et flumina Croesi,
dicat 'De nostro surge, poeta, toro.'
nam mea cum recitat, dicit se odisse beatos:
carmina tam sancte nulla puella colit.
multum in amore fides, multum constantia prodest:
qui dare multa potest, multa et amare potest.
seu mare per longum mea cogitet ire puella,
hanc sequar et fidos una aget aura duos.
unum litus erit sopitis unaque tecto
arbor, et ex una saepe bibemus aqua,
et tabula una duos poterit componere amantis,
prora cubile mihi seu mihi puppis erit.
omnia perpetiar: saeuus licet urgeat Eurus,
uelaque in incertum frigidus Auster agat,
quicumque et uenti miserum uexastis Ulixem,
et Danaum Euboico litore mille ratis,
et qui mouistis duo litora, cum ratis Argo
dux erat ignoto missa columba mari.
illa meis tantum non umquam desit ocellis,
incendat nauem Iuppiter ipse licet.
certe isdem nudi pariter iactabimur oris:
me licet unda ferat, te modo terra tegat.
sed non Neptunus tanto crudelis amori,
Neptunus fratri par in amore Ioui:
testis Amymone, latices dum ferret, in aruis
compressa, et Lernae pulsa tridente palus;
iam deus amplexu uotum persoluit, at illi
aurea diuinas urna profudit aquas.

crudelem et Borean rapta Orithyia negauit:
    hic deus et terras et maria alta domat.
crede mihi, nobis mitescet Scylla, nec umquam
    alternante uacans uasta Charybdis aqua;
ipsaque sidera erunt nullis obscura tenebris,
    purus et Orion, purus et Haedus erit.
quod mihi si ponenda tuo sit corpore uita,
    exitus hic nobis non inhonestus erit.

Heart of my heart, I dreamed I saw you shipwrecked,
I saw your weakening hands clutch at the air;
I heard you gasp that you had done me evil;
I saw you dragged down by your brine-soaked hair,
and tossed like Helle on the purple waters—
Helle, who slipped from ram's back into sea.
And terror shook me lest your name be given
that gulf, and sailors mourn your memory.
I prayed to Castor and Pollux, prayed to Neptune,
to mortal Ino now immortal made—
but in my dreams your flailing arms grew feeble;
your voice that called my name—I heard it fade.
If he had seen your eyes, the sea god Glaucus,
he would have seized and kept you for his own.
How envious they would have been, the sea nymphs,
their loveliness surpassed by yours alone!
But as you sank, I saw a dolphin swimming,
Arion's lute bearer, your guide to shore,
and I, prepared to leap and die beside you,
felt terror fade, for I could bear no more.

2.26b

Cynthia's mine! At this let all men marvel,
and through the city let my fame be spread!
Though emperors seek her and though Croesus beckon,
she will not turn a poet from her bed.
She says she scorns all wealth, having my verses—
no woman ever reverenced poetry more.
True hearts are constant; he who wins by bribing
may have a hundred light loves at his door.
Sail to Cathay, sweetheart, and I shall follow—

we're one, and the same breeze shall fill our sail,
the same shore give us rest, the same tree shade us,
the same spring quench our thirst and never fail.
Who cares how narrow is the bed we lie on,
whether it's at the ship's prow or the stern?
I can bear anything, even though storm winds force us
far from our course, with small hope of return—
like those that drove Ulysses to disaster
and wrecked the Greek fleet in the angry seas,
or those that carried Jason north, a white dove
guiding him through the cleft Symplegades.
May Juppiter himself kindle our vessel
as long as you remain within my sight!
and if we drown, may the waves take my body,
but on yours, washed ashore, the earth lie light.
Who frowns on love like ours? Not Neptune, surely,
who was, in love, the equal of heaven's king:
Amymone lay with him in the meadows
when he had pledged the drought-worn land a spring—
and, having had her, he redeemed his promise:
a golden urn poured forth the magic stream.
And Orithyia, ravished by the North Wind,
would not condemn him, brutal though he seem.
O we could tame even the monster Scylla,
could even charm Charybdis into rest!
No clouds shall mask the stars that ride above us—
Orion's path be clear from east to west.
And if death find me on your body lying,
where would I find a worthier way of dying?

(Carrier's translation)

Most modern editors (Richardson being a notable exception) begin a new elegy at line 21. Carrier's translation, printed here, following Butler's Loeb edition of 1912, creates a new poem there. Camps begins a third poem at line 29, where Barber is content to show a lacuna. Rothstein, following Scaliger and some late manuscripts, adds the next poem to the end of this one. In addition, editors have transposed lines in both parts of the poem. These divisions are contrary to the one given in the manuscripts, all of which except *N* print it as one elegy, *N* dividing at line 29 with Camps. No manuscripts divide at line 21. While *N* is our oldest manuscript, the division of elegies in it is occasionally confused as in all Propertian manuscripts (White, "Structure" 254), and before we can divide the poem, we need to examine both halves of it to see whether there is a connection between the two.

It used to be fashionable to discuss only lines 1–20, and Papanghelis (80–111) has recently offered a discussion of only lines 21–56, which he considers a complete poem. But scholars such as Williams, Macleod, and Wiggers have indicated enough connections between the parts of the poem to establish unity, and we can see the piece, with Richardson (286) and Alfonsi (44–45, although he divides the poem), as two dreams which balance each other. Lefèvre also sees a balance between two "visions" of "danger" and characterizes the piece as an "internal monologue" with "associative structure" (Lefèvre, "Properziana" 45–51).[6] Wiggers suggests a place to look for the alluring attraction of the poem:

> The mythological allusions are also extremely elaborate, and Propertius' inclination to linger sensuously over every descriptive detail is frustrating to the reader of this suspenseful tale. Lines 5 and 6, for instance, betray an almost painterly pleasure in the contrast between the color of the sea (*purpureis fluctibus*) and the fleece (*aurea ouis*) and between the textures of the water (the turbulence of which is implied in *agitatam*) and the soft wool (*molli tergore*), which is inappropriate to the danger being described. (123)

Wiggers adds more details, and scholars such as Quinn (*Explorations* 191, 195) have noted the use of color in line 16 as well as in lines 5–6, but the point should be obvious: Propertius wishes the reader to see, to hear, to taste, to smell, and to feel the scene he is describing. The poem is an excellent example of the imagist style.

One of the most perceptive critics on this poem is Rothstein. In spite of his textual surgery, he notes that the poem is dominated by visual images from pictorial art, to the detriment of rational structure, and by other visual effects such as color. In his comments on 2.26 and on his 2.26b (our 2.26.21–2.27.16), he speaks of "a row of pictures" and of "fantasy" (374, 375, 377, 378); Lefèvre compares this pictorial style to that of modernist interior monologues ("Properziana" 50–51).[7] Much of this imagist atmosphere is created by the image of Helle, which in turn governs the entire dream picture. It has been recognized for more than a century that Propertius' description of Helle is based upon representations of the scene in pictorial art (Helbig 119–20; Otto, "Particula Prior" 16; Keyssner 280–81; Camps). The fullest description has been offered by Margaret Hubbard (164, 166–168, 173), who notes the color effects in lines 5–6 and 16 and refers to some pictures of Helle printed in Roscher (3: 2, 2466). Clearly, as Hubbard argues, the elements in these pictures govern the structure of the dream, although the dream, as a dream should, is presented in associative fashion, as the poet recoils back and forth from pictorial details to his personal, psychological reactions to the scene. In lines 1–2 the poet describes the scene; in the second couplet we see his reaction (jealousy). The third couplet shifts to myth and pictorial art (Helle), the fourth again to his reaction (fear that the same fate as befell Helle will befall Cynthia). Lines 9–10 shift this fear to a different mythological plane: "I should have prayed," the poet thinks. Lines 11–12 return to narration, although still within the scene as portrayed in the murals of Helle, lines 13–16 again to the world of myth. In lines 17 and 18 the dolphin enters (narration) sparking the final reaction of the speaker in lines 19–20: a foiled attempt to jump and rescue. Hubbard emphasizes that the moist hair, the rocks, the extended hands, all the elements in the murals, are there in the poem and that the details are not presented rationally, as dreams demand no reason, but rather as a viewer would see the same details in the ancient paintings. Propertius transfers the contemplative process to a dreamworld and provides a "frustration dream" that Freud would gladly have analyzed (in fact a Freudian interpretation of the dream may be found in Sullivan, *Propertius* 100). We have one large-scale image, the drowning scene, with an associative structure governing the description.

This still does not account for the second part of the poem. In his commentary Butler, who saw it as necessary to divide the poem, also saw one way in which it could be unified: lines 1–20 are an assertion of faith on the part of the poet (*Opera* 234). The main stumbling block to this is the "nunc" ("now") in line 21, but there is no reason why we cannot translate the word literally and interpret it as Muecke does the same word at Vergil, *Eclogue* 10.24: "*Nunc* in 44 signals a return to reality after a day-dream" (7.10; cf. Williams, *Figures* 130). The rest of the poem after line 21, then, can be seen as a rational response to the dominating image of lines 1–20, although it, too, is visual (Papanghelis 101–10). In support of this argument we should also consider the geography of lines 37–40. The "Euboicum litus" ("Euboean shore") of line 28 and the "duo litora" ("two shores") of line 39 seem to refer to the eastern and western boundaries of the Ionian Sea; between them is the Hellespont (Butler-Barber; Camps). The speaker is particularly worried about the area in which Helle's accident, and by implication Cynthia's accident in the dream, was supposed to have occurred. This also connects the dream to the final thirty-eight lines of the poem. Finally, the poem ends with an unusual couplet. "Quod mihi si ponenda tuo sit corpore uita" ("but if my life should be ended on your body") is unique Latin; Richardson calls the line "vivid, even macabre" (289; cf. Papanghelis 126). It creates a striking image. One more reason for this phrasing may be suggested. The "uita" ("life") here is perhaps intended to be a repetition of the "uita" in line 1 but with an entirely different meaning. Thus the poem exhibits the familiar ring-composition so characteristic of Propertius, especially in poems with difficult structures.

This poem, then, combines all of the traits discussed in this chapter and in chapter 2. It has an associative structure; we should note immediately the changes of address, emotion, and theme, although the sections are bound by ring-composition and by thematic ties into a coherent unit. It exhibits the kind of dramatic unity that scholars have observed in other poems. Godolphin argued this kind of construction for Propertius 1.8, 1.15, 2.24, and 2.28, as well as for several other poems in Catullus, Tibullus, and Horace. White has also argued for "dramatic unity" in Propertius 1.8, 2.28, 2.29, 2.33, 2.34, and 3.20 ("Structure"; "Dramatic Unity"; "Unity" 63–72). The structure, then, need not disturb us, especially in light of the presentation of associative structure in chapter 2. The first part of the poem is an imagist dream, but the second part of the poem leaps from subconscious dream to conscious, rational musing about the dream. We might appeal again to Pound's concept of the superposition of narrative on image (or vice versa) applied to Propertius 1.3 earlier in this chapter. Here the second part of the poem, the poet's reaction, is superposed on the dream image. What we have is an image with first a suprarational and then a rational reaction to it, although there are still associative and imagistic elements in the second part of the poem. The idyllic, almost pastoral scenes in lines 29–36 come immediately to mind. The confusing order of these lines (the lovers are first on a ship, then on a shore, then on a ship again) has caused consternation among more traditional critics; Housman's attempt to rationalize the passage through emendation and transposition, discussed in chapter 1, is a good example. But Propertius' intent is clearly to present three vignettes, all highly visual. We see even the details of scenery and the sleeping arrangements. Papanghelis (86–88) has called attention to the visuality in the "love-death" scene in line 43. Similarly the mythology in lines 37–56 would have created visual associations for contemporary readers; Butler-Barber on lines 47–50 suggest an artistic model for Amymone, and there is a portrait of Neptune and Amymone's embrace preserved on a mural in the House of the Vettii, reproduced for example in Lenz' commentary on Ovid's *Amores*. Finally the poem ends with a striking image, as we have seen. Still, the entire first part of the poem is dominated by image and subconscious association, or at least by the intent to create an appearance of such.

There is more than a superficial similarity between the techniques attributed to Propertius in the last three chapters and twentieth-century imagism (Coffman; Materer; Robinson). The imagist movement was more or less invented, with stimulus from Bergson and the French symbolists, by T. E. Hulme, named ("Imagisme") by Ezra Pound, and popularized by Amy Lowell. Pound soon left the movement in favor of vorticism, a movement more oriented toward the visual arts and led by Pound and the artist-writer Wyndham Lewis, but even T. S. Eliot is associated with the mainstream members such as Aldington, H.D. (Hilda Doolittle), and Flint. There has been some discussion about the distinction between imagism and vorticism. Recently Robinson has argued that "there is no difference between Imagism and Vorticism"; rather "Imagism would become merely the literary element in 'Vorticism,' a new movement uniting all the art forms . . ." (208, 191). Although imagism meant many things to many people, it was characterized by the cultivation of the image rather than the abstraction as the most essential part of cognition and hence of poetic communication. The members tended to avoid wordiness and decoration and instead to cultivate metaphor and concision. One cannot read such statements in the context of classical literature without thinking of Propertius, who, as Pound recognized, reacted against the public style of his contemporaries and instead presented images from his own private experience. The similarity between such poems as Propertius 1.3 or 2.26 and Pound's short haiku poems has already been noted. It has also been mentioned that some see Pound as a Lockean reaction against the classicism of the Renaissance; Propertius, then, is reacting against classicism at its source, against the rationally distilled presentation of experience. Propertius aims to communicate raw experience itself on a suprarational level. One can see why the classicist Quintilian preferred Tibullus and why modern classicists prefer to emend and transpose. But Propertius' decision was not to write in the standard classical mode. The philosophic and generic background behind this decision is the subject of the next chapter. Margaret Hubbard, who thinks imagism common in Books III and IV of Propertius, finds Callimachean "some aspects of his style in Book II, particularly in its use of a series of flashing and distinct images" (168). Callimachus may have provided an impetus, but we shall see that the Propertian poetics embraces a much larger nexus of literary and philosophical theories.

5
Propertius' Poetics of Imagism

At this point I might seem to have committed the "chronological fallacy." The modernist theories presented in the preceding chapters come not from classical writers, but from nineteenth-century thinkers. The theories of psychological time and of imagistic cognition were developed largely by Henri Bergson and William James, the theory of the stream of consciousness and of the subconscious by James and by Sigmund Freud. One must ask how Propertius himself viewed the process of mental perception, and whether or not this might have influenced his approach to poetics.

One very popular psychological theory in antiquity was thoroughly imagistic. Democritus, the founder of the atomic school, explained perception and cognition in terms of atomic "images," which he called εἴδωλα; for the atomist perception and cognition must be atomic, since all that exist are atoms and the void. Democritus developed a very influential theory; Windelband's account is worth quoting at length:

> This *theory of images* appeared very plausible to ancient thought. It brought to definite expression, and indeed to a certain extent explained, the mode of representing things which is still common for the ordinary consciousness, as if our perception were "copies" of things existing outside of us. . . . This theory at once attained the predominance in physiological psychology, and retained its position until after the beginnings of modern philosophy, where it was defended by Locke. (1: 114, Windelband's italics)

And with Locke we are of course on the verge of modern associationist theory; Yvor Winters comments about Pound that "the structure [namely, of the *Cantos*] appears to be that of more or less free association, or progression through reverie. Sensory perception replaces idea. Pound, early in his career, adopted the inversion derived from Locke by the associationists: since all ideas arise from sensory impressions, all ideas can be expressed in terms of sensory impressions" (*Function* 47). The poetics of Pound or Joyce might seem far too sophisticated to be applied to Propertius, but that is only because it is based upon a more sophisticated theory of the image—Locke, James, Bergson, Freud, and so on, rather than upon Democritus.

Propertius would of course have had access to the imagist theory of perception and cognition through Lucretius' *De Rerum Natura*, the long Epicurean poem written at about the time Propertius was born in the mid-first century B.C. Book IV of that poem explains these processes in detail. Lucretius explains how the *imagines* (images, his word for the Democritean εἴδωλα) are small layers that leave objects and strike the eyes, passing thence in image form to the brain (a theory not unlike the modern one, although in modern theory of course the images do not retain their original form as they pass to the brain; rather the brain unscrambles the messages). Lucretius accounts for deceptions in vision and for how the visual impressions stimulate motion, erotic impulses, and so on. To the modern reader it is astounding how this very flexible theory can account for virtually all spheres of experience. Most relevant for us, perhaps, is Lucretius' discussion of dreams at 4.722–776. Dream visions are also thin images but ones that have become conflated and cannot be separated from reality by the sleeping mind. The dreaming mind sees a series of images that create an impression of movement, just as the modern motion picture has still images quickly succeed each other to create an illusion of movement.

But there is also implied in these passages an Epicurean theory of imagination. To Lucretius, imagination would be the gathering of images by the mind into new forms and would involve the disregarding of rational judgments commanded by what we call reality. There is nothing unusual in this; the appearance of the word *image* in the English word *imagination*, both derived from the Latin word *imago*, shows that our own conception of imagination is strongly visual, derived perhaps from the Epicurean tradition. Lucretius does not explain what happens when one reads or writes poetry or even what happens when one sees a painting or statue. But I suspect that he would view all three activities as essentially similar processes and perhaps would compare them to the imaginative free play of dreams. Certainly Propertius would have done so. Cynthia appears to Propertius, in the visual terms of pictorial art, in a dream in 2.26 (analyzed in the previous chapter); her ghost appears to him in a dream in 4.7; and there are numerous blendings of poetic image and pictorial image—if indeed with Propertius we can ever make such a distinction. Propertius appears to create in his poetry the image as though, as described by Lucretius, it were the most effective way to stimulate his reader's thought processes. This description obviously is not far from the poetics of Pound. In any case, the Lucretian poem is at least one source from which Propertius could have developed an imagist poetics, much as the modernists developed it from Locke's similar, if more complex, theory.

It might be objected immediately that Lucretius, although an Epicurean, is no imagist, and that Propertius, even if an imagist, is no Epicurean. But an imagist poetics would explain one well-known feature of Lucretius' style, that being his excellent use of description, especially of natural scenes.[1] It is worth mentioning here that the original impulse behind imagism, as conceived by T. E. Hulme, was the capturing of the essences of concrete, physical objects. Lucretius does not explain how poetry works, nor evidently did Epicurus or any of Lucretius' sources. There is a good reason for this: the Epicureans were opposed to the writing of poetry, which to them was not capable of communicating philosophical truth; for this reason some have questioned the orthodoxy of Lucretius' Epicureanism (de Lacy).

As to Propertius' Epicureanism, first he need not have adopted the Epicurean philosophy in toto in order to take inspiration from its theory of images. Second, Propertius was acquainted with the Epicurean and Stoic disputes, and he also knew the intricacies of the doctrine of images (Thomas K. Hubbard; Disch 48, 52–53; Alfonsi 62–63; Papanghelis 207–10), and Papanghelis has pointed to some interesting parallels between Propertius and Lucretius. At 2.34.27–28 he seems to take a verbal jab at Lucretius' treatise *De Rerum Natura*:

> *Quid tua Socraticis tibi nunc sapientia libris*
> *proderit aut rerum dicere posse uias?*
>
> What good is Socrates and all that wisdom
> that tells us why the world is as it is?
>
> (Carrier's translation)

At 3.21.25–26, where Propertius contemplates a trip to Athens as an escape from his life and love in Rome, the speaker alludes to Epicurus by name:

> *illinc uel stadiis animum emendare Platonis*
> *incipiam, aut hortis, docte Epicure, tuis?*
>
> The Academia will cleanse my spirit;
> You, Epicurus, you will clear my mind.
>
> (Carrier's translation)

This passage raises what is perhaps the greatest difficulty in attributing Epicurean ideas to Propertius. Epicureanism advocates a life of contemplation (as in the master's famous garden, alluded to here) and de-emphasizes sex as a pain rather than a pleasure (cf. Disch 53). Lucretius argues at length for sexual abstinence in Book IV. The essentially sexual nature of Propertius' way of life is inimical to Epicureanism (at least as it is explained by Lucretius; other Epicureans may have been less stringent with regard to sex). Both Epicureanism and Propertius' way of life are aspects of the vita passiva but quite different aspects.

This objection that Propertius' values are antithetical to Epicureanism is worthy of further discussion. Boucher (30–32) has considered the fundamental similarity between the elegiac life of *otium* (leisure) and the Epicurean life of ἀταραξία (a word that is difficult to translate but indicates intellectual peace of mind). The essential problem to Boucher in ascribing Epicureanism to Propertius is that the Epicurean life of social withdrawal appealed to those without property and social standing and hence social obligations. The upper classes were drawn to Stoicism, which acknowledged social responsibilities. But Boucher notes also that the Epicurean ideal of φιλία (friendship) furnished an ideal of the smaller social unit that became common especially during the civil wars, when the larger social structure weakened; Boucher cites as examples of such the neoterics of Catullus' time and the circle of Maecenas, which of course included Propertius, but he adds that the Epicureanism of these groups can scarcely be called pure Epicureanism, since the elegists were "believing in the value of the arts, in that of love as a form of life" (31).[2] Tait, furthermore, has shown that the circle of Maecenas developed out of the Neapolitan group of Epicureans with Philodemus (108–18). There is, then, a very general sense in which Propertius could be considered an Epicurean.

In contrast, the poetic genre generally associated with Epicureanism is bucolic or pastoral, and Tibullus, rather than Propertius, is generally considered the pastoral elegist.[3] It seems that this blending of pastoral and elegy was conceived by Messala and developed by Cornelius Gallus, if we can trust Vergil's picture of that poet.[4] But Propertius also shares some of the traits associated by Walker with Epicurean pastoral. The friendship (φιλία) was offered to the poet by the circle of Maecenas, as was noted above, but even more so by the group of characters, whether real, fictional, or a combination of both, addressed and discussed in Propertius' poetry. Bright, in his discussion of Tibullus, categorizes as "bucolic" the "haze over his [Tibullus'] perceptions (and ours)" (4). The same sort of "haze" is generated by Propertius' flights of fancy into the realms of dream image and mythology. Postgate, in the introduction to his *Select Elegies*, suggested a similar effect when he commented that "the habit of vagueness which I have already touched upon is now [namely, while "awakening sympathy"] most effective. It adds a softness and gentleness to the forms that he would bring before us, and wraps them, as it were, in a floating golden haze" (lxxvii); Krókowsky sees the function of nature in Catullus, Horace, and pastoral poetry as transferred in elegy to mythology, pictorial arts, and "urban" pursuits. Bright emphasizes the ties of Propertius to the "real world," but actually the stylistic and structural effects discussed in chapters 2, 3, and 4 serve to place Propertius in a poetic sphere almost as unreal as Tibullus'. The reader of Propertius spends time not in the mainstream of Roman life but in the imagination of a poet who avoids that mainstream and locates his poems outside of it. The scene of the poems is not the forum but the bedroom, or even the bedroom as perceived by Propertius, and that bedroom is a place disassociated from the forum; it is, in fact, the pastoral scene, the *locus amoenus* (pleasant place). Guillemin has shown that both Tibullus and Propertius create emotive settings; in Tibullus the setting is provided by pastoral scenes, but in Propertius it is provided by mythology, and especially by mythological scenes from pictorial art. Propertius' pastoral scenes do not occur in the country and do not involve *pastores* (shepherds), but rather Propertius' poetic talent, like Catullus', flourishes in the city (106–8).[5] His poetry, when pastoral in the broader sense of the term, we need to characterize as "urban pastoral," the retreat from the public life of the city to the private life of the city.

One more Epicurean tie to Propertius remains to be investigated. The mainstream Epicureans left us little poetic theory. But we do have fragmentary remains of a very interesting treatise, *On Poems* (Περὶ Ποιημάτων), written by the Epicurean Philodemus.[6] Although there is no evidence that Propertius had read Philodemus' treatise, Philodemus spent considerable time in Rome (slightly before Propertius' arrival there) and the latter's epigrams in Greek had a considerable influence upon Propertius (Tait).

Philodemus contends that in poetry form and content are inseparable: "In fact Neoptolemus taught incorrectly to sever the combination of language from the thoughts" (translation mine).[7]

In terms of classical poetic theory this distinction is unique. Philodemus believes that the slightest change in the form (words) will result in alteration of the content; Greenberg illustrates, following a papyrus published separately, that Philodemus even opposes "poetic metathesis, i.e., changing the order of the words in poetry": "They are accustomed to present innumerable verses, such as those of Homer and the other epics, which differ according to the variations. However, we must assert that the thought becomes better or worse through the metatheses" (Greenberg's translation, "Metathesis," 267). De Lacy demonstrates one more matter of relevance. In general the Epicureans avoided poetry because poetry and poetic language appeal to the passions rather than to the reason, but Philodemus, by advocating the blending of form and content, advocates a blending of emotion and reason into a unity that, as a final product, can be judged by the reason as a work of art (87–89).

We have stumbled upon a theory of imitation but a theory different from any other in the ancient world.[8] To Philodemus, poetry does not imitate actual life. He informs us in the *Rhetoric* that "any 'imitation' of things by words is impossible" (Hubbell's translation, 294), a sentiment repeated often in *On Poems*, nor should the poet imitate famous authors, as the contemporary theory of *imitatio* (imitation) recommended.[9] What, then, should the poet imitate? De Lacy focuses our attention in the right direction: "By imitation they [namely, the Epicureans] mean the reflection of the intellectual material in the emotional" (90). In other words, the proper fitting of form to content, as discussed above, yields the proper imitation; the form, strictly speaking, should imitate the content. Hence the literary work is to be judged by the success of the imitation, in this strict sense. This, then, is at least one formulation of the Epicurean theory of literary imitation.

Obviously one way in which form could imitate content would be through imagism, although there are only hints of this in the fragments of Philodemus. He does speak of "the imagistic art" (τῆς εἰκαστικῆς, Jensen 2.15–18, with τέχνη supplied in Jensen's "Wortregister"). This phrase has a long history, stemming from Plato. McKeon interprets a passage in Plato's *Sophist* (235B–236C): "Man likewise makes things which are, and he makes images. His imitative or image-making art (εἰδωλοποιικὴ τέχνη) is divided into two parts, the copymaking art (εἰκαστική), which follows its original in length, breadth, depth, and color, and the fantastic art (φανταστική), in which truth is abandoned and the images are given, not their actual proportions, but such proportions as seem beautiful" (154). In Plato the images imitate the Forms or actual existences; for the Epicurean Philodemus, the images (εἰκάσματα, or εἴδωλα) can only have the meaning that *imago* (image) had for Lucretius.

Yet more promising is Philodemus' insistence upon ἐνάργεια, translated by Liddell-Scott-Jones-McKenzie as "clear and distinct perception" (556): "What necessity is there to describe an action distinctly and tersely, when many not only lies but also mythological things are described most distinctly among the poets?" (translation mine).[10] Wilkinson comments on this passage that "he not only rejects the idea that they must be 'true to life,' but almost forestalls Philostratus in naming 'imagination'" (150). And it seems that, perhaps for the first time in the ancient world, a poetics is being developed that judges poetry on the quality of the imitation as a work of art, rather than as a reflection of the actual worldly state of affairs. Consequently Rostagni has suggested that Philodemus was an expositor of an aesthetic like Croce's, according to which poetry is divorced from pragmatic ends and is judged by intuition; Croce's views on Propertius have been discussed already, but it is worth adding here that with Crocean aesthetics we are again in the midst of an imagist poetics, for Crocean intuition works primarily through images.[11]

One worthwhile question about Propertius and Philodemus has not been asked. Propertius took inspiration from the epigrams of Philodemus in *The Greek Anthology*, but what similarity is there between Propertius and Philodemus in terms of the stylistic and especially structural anomalies noted in the last three chapters? One of Philodemus' epigrams (5.4) addresses three different audiences (Philainis, Xantho, and the bed) in the short space of six lines; two poems (5.46 and 3.570) are written in dialogues, a structural device perhaps too radical even for Propertius, although this may explain at least in part the curious poem Propertius 4.1, in which the speaker addresses and then receives an extended reply from his astrologer Horos, and also the dialogic elements in Propertius noted by Tränkle (143–49). Another poem (5.306) is written in the persona of a girl, and one poem that might be by Philodemus (5.308) contains imagined negative responses on the part of a female addressee. This last poem definitely anticipates (if it is not spurious and does not postdate Propertius) the Roman poet's use of dramatic structure. One final poem (5.112) will be quoted in full:

> I loved. Who hath not? I made revels in her honor. Who is uninitiated in those mysteries? But I was distraught. By whom? Was it not by a god? Good bye to it; for already the grey locks hurry on to replace the black, and tell me I have reached the age of discretion. While it was playtime I played; now it is over. I will turn to more worthy thoughts. (Paton's translation, 1: 181)

Here the speaker's dialogue with himself appears to me similar to the interior monologue in Propertius.

That Propertius 1.3 is based on Philodemus 5.123, as scholars generally agree (Baker, "Beauty" 245–46), leaves little doubt that Propertius read and was influenced by Philodemus' poetry. Whether or not he read *On Poems* probably can never be determined, and some might find my speculations here extreme. But my point is that Propertius could have found the raw materials of imagism in Epicurean documents, and doubtless he had many more such documents than we. In addition, modernist theorists often mention Lucretius. One of Bergson's earliest works was a study of Lucretius, now partially available in English translation, in which he suggested that the Roman poet possessed the same intuitive grasp of the world that has become the basis of the interior monologue (*Philosophy*); Freud quoted Lucretius in the beginning of *The Interpretation of Dreams* (4: 1, 8–9); and Virginia Woolf's words describing modern fiction will bear repetition: "Let us record the atoms as they fall upon the mind in the order in which they fall, let us trace the pattern, however disconnected and incoherent in appearance, which each sight or incident scores upon the consciousness" (190). Friedman compares Woolf's thinking here to expressionist painting, but what else is a painting by Seurat but an atomist image? An influence of atomism upon imagism, in Propertius and in the twentieth century, seems difficult to deny.

Even if Propertius took no note of contemporary epistemological theory, which I think is highly unlikely, the raw materials of an imagist poetics would have been available to him from the standard Peripatetic teachings on poetics. I refer here of course to the famous doctrine of *ut pictura poesis* (poetry is like painting). This doctrine appears in nearly every classical discussion of the nature of poetry. Simonides was credited by Plutarch (*Moralia* 346F–347A) with the earliest comparison of poetry and the visual arts, and Horace popularized the doctrine in his *Ars Poetica* (1–37, 361–65), but it was Aristotle who gave the doctrine its most coherent theoretical formulation.[12]

Plato had compared literature and the visual arts in order to disparage the former on epistemological grounds. To Aristotle, who wished to justify or at least explain the nature of the aesthetic experience, the two types of arts were also nearly identical. Comparisons of poetry and painting or sculpture permeate the *Poetics*. In the first chapter Aristotle used the comparison to show how arts can be distinguished "by differences in their objects, or in the manner of their imitations": "Just as colour and form are used as means by some, who (whether by art or constant practice) imitate and portray many things by their aid, and the voice is used by others; so also in the above-mentioned group of arts, the means as a whole with them are rhythm, language, and harmony—used, however, either singly or in certain combinations" (1447a, Bywater's translation). In chapter 2 of the *Poetics*, Aristotle informs us of an interesting corollary to his contention that poetry and painting share the same "object":

> The objects the imitator represents are actions, with agents who are necessarily either good men or bad—the diversities of human character being nearly always derivative from this distinction, since the line between virtue and vice is one dividing the whole of mankind. It follows, therefore, that the agents represented must be either above our own level of goodness, or beneath it, or just such as we are; in the same way as, with the painters, the personages of Polygnotus are better than we are, those of Pauson worse, and those of Dionysius just like ourselves. (1448a, Bywater's translation)

To Aristotle, then, the two types of art involve similar aesthetic principles and, we would suspect, even call for similar techniques of artistic creation and of artistic judgment.

The assumption of such similarity came to dominate classical and neoclassical artistic theory. The comparison of painting and oratory is frequent in the Greek and Roman rhetorical criticism of Cicero and his contemporaries, and in the Renaissance, for example, painters were expected to follow the doctrine of the unities. Lessing, in his *Laocoon*, is generally credited with demonstrating the inadequacy of the artistic principles behind the doctrine of *ut pictura poesis*. Lessing made two points of critical importance. First, he showed that the two types of art do not have the same object of imitation, since poetry is in actuality a temporal medium, while painting is spatial: "Subjects which, or the various parts of which, exist side by side, may be called *bodies*. Consequently, bodies with their visible properties form the proper subjects of painting. Subjects which or the various parts of which succeed each other may in general be called *actions*. Consequently, actions form the proper subjects of poetry" (55, his italics). Second, as a consequence of this difference in medium, the goals of the two types of art are also different. Poetry should depict action and character, while painting, which can depict neither action nor character, should depict beauty.

Actually these ideas are not original with Lessing and can be observed in part at least in Leonardo da Vinci (Lee 251–52), in Castelvetro (Weinberg 369), in Plutarch (*Moralia* 346F–347A), in Dio Chrysostom (*Oratio* 12.70), and in Xenophon (*Memorabilia*

3.10.1–8). That is not really important. What is important is that Lessing specified what must have been a real problem to the practicing poet or painter following the doctrine of *ut pictura poesis*: poetry is not like painting. No amount of description, metaphor, or other stylistic technique can create the visual effects of painting, and no special effects in painting can create exactly the narrative effect of literature.

The twentieth century has seen countless attempts to deny this difference between the arts, we might almost say to refute Lessing and restore the doctrine of *ut pictura poesis*. We have seen Duchamp, for example, attempt to break the temporal limits of painting with his *Nude Descending a Staircase*, although the result there is self-conscious art rather than a genuine illusion of passing time. The reunification of the spatial and temporal arts is also one of the chief goals of modernism. Imagism, that movement shared by writers and pictorial artists, comes quickly to mind, but even James Joyce tried to unify the two spheres of experience while alluding to the Lessing passage quoted above. In *A Portrait of the Artist as a Young Man*, Stephen suggests, while explaining his aesthetic purportedly drawn from Aquinas, that the primary aesthetic step, "integritas," involves the separation of the aesthetic object from space or time, that is, transcending the artistic medium (212); in the Proteus episode of *Ulysses*, Stephen walks with closed eyes through the realms of space and time together, "a very short space of time through a very short time of space" (37).[13] Once again against neoclassicism Propertius and modernism join hands.

This difficulty for the artist explains why critics have found so much classical poetic theory irrelevant to classical literature. The *Ars Poetica* does not help very much with the interpretation of the *Odes*, nor with many other classical literary works. Yet one exception can be pointed to, and that is the elegies of Propertius. Almost alone among the Greek and Roman poets, Propertius attempts a serious application of the techniques of painting to the writing of poetry, as can be seen especially in the poems analyzed in chapter 4. In the dream of 2.26, Propertius presents an almost completely static picture, and the only action is the psychological action on the part of the speaker. In 1.3 three entirely static pictures appear rapidly, leaving the reader and the speaker of the poem gazing at the static Cynthia. Lessing would have said that the reader is observing the unmoving beauty of Cynthia, that Propertius represents an object rather than an action. At the end of the poem, of course, Cynthia springs into action and destroys the beauty the reader has observed. Propertius 2.2 presents a slightly different but more typical case. There, as we saw, a variety of pictures pass before the reader, who must assimilate them and make them coherent. The connections between the pictures are merely associative, and the effect is more like a tour of an art gallery as the speaker reflects, in monologue, upon each picture than like the usual classical poem. This practice is in fact the same as we observed, on a less pictorial and more thematic level, in the poems in chapter 2, where the standard classical notions of structure and narrative have broken down and ideas are connected only associatively.

Probably no aesthetic theory can account for all of Propertius' poetic goals and methods. He is an experimental poet, attempting to gain effect through violations of some of the normal classical notions of style and structure and through exaggerations of others. This chapter has approached Propertius through Greek and Roman theories of imagery. Propertius cannot have been completely ignorant of these and similar theories that were available in the standard classical handbooks and treatises on philosophy, literature, and rhetoric. In the application of these theories, Propertius reveals himself as a poet worthy of serious study and reflection. He also reveals himself as similar to the modernists, writers who also strive for effect by applying psychological theory as well as the methods of the pictorial arts to literature.

I must close with a clarification. Clearly Propertius, like Pound, was struck by the role of images in the creation and transmission of poetic material. This does not imply that imagism seems necessarily an ideal or even desirable manner of writing. I have attempted not to assert judgments on the success or failure of imagism (either Propertian or modernist). What is important to realize is that both modern imagists and Propertius believed in the image and employed it within very loose, nonrational, or better, suprarational, structures. For the modern imagists this was a reaction against classicism; for Propertius it was a reaction against the classical principles of his contemporaries. This is probably, as Postgate suggested, why he found fewer admirers than Tibullus in Quintilian's time, and it is also, I suspect, why Pound asserted that Propertius' situation in the Roman empire mirrored his own in the First World War. Both wrote private poetry of retreat rather than public poetry of social participation. The imagist style of Propertius, in fact, provided the perfect medium to convey the ideals of what I have called the urban pastoral, and his poetics had popular bases in Epicurean epistemology and ethics and in Peripatetic aesthetics upon which to rest.

6
Propertius in the Renaissance and Beyond

J. Wright Duff, in his history of Latin literature, closes his discussion of Propertius with a few comments on his literary impact after the time of Apuleius: "Then, from the time of Justinian I, when the Greek epigrammatist Paullus Silentiarius, imitated him, till the days of Petrarch, Propertius is as good as unknown. But, since the Renaissance, he has been sure of recognition, though not always of recognition as high as he deserves" (422).[1] Duff is certainly correct in asserting the lack of Propertian allusions in the Middle Ages; indeed many would even take away Paullus, claiming him to be instead an imitator of Propertius' sources rather than of Propertius. I noted in chapter 1 that many scholars have tried to trace the history of Propertius' manuscripts in the medieval period, arguing that the grammarians were citing from a five-book edition (or rather from a four-book edition comprised of our Books II–IV with Book II separated). But now Menes has examined those grammarians and concluded that there is no sure proof that the grammarians were citing from Propertius as a primary source. It seems that Propertius disappeared for nearly seven centuries, until near the end of the twelfth century; he may have been read by Carolingian writers such as Ermoldus or Alcuin, but the earliest medieval author who certainly read Propertius was John of Salisbury, who died in 1180, shortly before *N*, our oldest manuscript, was copied (Butrica, *Manuscript* 20–24). Soon after, Albert of Stade made obvious allusions to the text of Propertius in his epic *Troilus* (Crowley). And Duff is also correct in ascribing to Petrarch a leading role in the revival of Propertius, although, as we shall see, Propertius was not truly understood until the nineteenth century.

Ullman has explained the connection between Petrarch and Propertius' manuscripts ("Manuscripts"; *Studies* 49–50, 177–88), and there is no need to repeat the details here. He clearly owned his own copy, which is now lost but was a member of the *AFLP* family of manuscripts. Ullman notes that Petrarch never mentions Propertius among his "favorite authors" and concludes "that Petrarch was not a great admirer of Propertius we can admit. That he read through his poems hastily, perhaps only once, we can also admit. Propertius did not belong to the small group of Petrarchan favorites" (*Studies* 177).

These last comments of Ullman are somewhat open to question. Ullman himself finds a quotation of Propertius in Petrarch's letter (*Familiares* 24.4.9–10) to Vergil, adding that Petrarch seems to use Donatus to correct his reading of Propertius 2.34.66; Ullman also finds notes on Propertius in Petrarch's Vergil manuscript and refers to allusions to Propertius found by various scholars in Petrarch's *Africa*, in his miscellaneous Latin poetry, and in *Rime* 1.35 (*Studies* 186–88; cf. Zingerle). Several other allusions to Propertius in the Italian poems are found in Muscetta's *La letteratura italiana*. It seems worth discussing at least one of these poems by Petrarch, *Canzioniere* 145, in order to see what has happened to Propertius:

Ponmi ove 'l sole occide i fiori e l'erba,
o dove vince lui il ghiaccio e la neve;
ponmi ov'è 'l carro suo temprato e leve,
et ov'è chi cel rende, o chi cel serba;
ponmi in umil fortuna, od in superba,
al dolce aere sereno, al fosco e greve;
ponmi a la nutte, al di'lungo ed al breve,
a la matura etate od a l'acerba;
ponmi in cielo, od in terra, od in abisso,
in alto poggio, in valle ima e palustre,

libero spirto, od a' suoi membri affisso;
    ponmi con fama oscura, o con illustre:
sarò qual fui, vivrò com'io son visso,
continuando il mio sospir trilustre.

(2:1, 305–6)

Put me where the sun destroys the flowers and the grass, or where the ice and the snow conquer it, put me where its chariot is tempered and light, and where is the one who restores that chariot, or who preserves it; put me in lowly fortune, or in high, in air which is sweet, serene, or in dark and heavy; put me among nights, either long or short, in the summer either late or difficult; put me in the sky, or on earth, or in the abyss, on top of a mountain, at the bottom of a valley or swamp, my spirit freed, or stuck to its members; put me with obscure reputation, or with a bright one: I shall be what I was, I shall live as I have lived, continuing my fifteen-day sigh. (translation mine)

Muscetta provides a suitable interpretation of this poem, providing a date, a metrical structure and a detailed analysis of the formal structure. What especially interests us here is the use of classical sources. Muscetta argues that the poem is an elaboration of the last eight lines of Horace, *Odes* 1.22.17–24, the famous poem that begins "integer uitae":

pone me pigris ubi nulla campis
arbor aestiva recreatue aura,
quod latus mundi nebulae malusque
    Iuppiter urget;

pone sub curru nimium propinqui
solis in terra domibus negata:
dulce ridentem Lalagen amabo,
    dulce loquentem.[2]

Put me where no tree is nourished by summer air upon stingy plains, that side of the world clouds and troublesome Jupiter press; put me in the chariot of the too neighboring sun upon a land denied to homes: sweetly laughing, sweetly speaking Lalage I shall love. (translation mine)

But Petrarch's poem is no longer about love, but rather about life in general. This effect Muscetta sees as enhanced by the other classical allusions in the text and particularly by the allusion in line 13 to Propertius 2.15.35, a line that also appears after a long *adynaton* or list of impossible situations (2: 1, 305):

> huius ero uiuus, mortuus huius ero
>
> hers I'll be alive, dead hers I'll be. (translation mine)

At first glance the argument for allusion does not appear very strong, until Muscetta makes the decisive point: "And one might see also how from the Propertian verse has been dropped in the translation the personal pronoun ("*huius*") to indicate that the passion and the calling of the spirit is not merely amatory" (2: 1, 306).[3] Petrarch has modified the Propertian passage the same way as he has the Horatian: he abstracts the erotic connotations out of the classical poets and makes them more reflective about the spiritual world in general. This change is of course typical not only of Petrarch but also of Renaissance writers in general. The classical poets are read, and they influence the Renaissance writers, but in the process they are transformed, in this case intentionally.

Due perhaps to Petrarch or to Salutati (who owned one of the extant manuscripts of the *AFLP* tradition), Propertius became very popular in Italian literature of the fifteenth century. Politian, for example, wrote Latin elegies in many ways reminiscent of Propertius, although his actual allusions are not as meaningful as Petrarch's. Much more fruitful is the study of the elegies written by Aeneas Silvius Piccolomini, which were given the title of *Cinthia*. Baca has studied the entire book, or at least its remains (after Piccolomini became Pope, the *Cinthia* understandably fell into low repute), and concluded that "Aeneas is indebted to his model for more than a title for his elegies, since his borrowings include direct adaptations, adroit echoings, and techniques of literary portraiture" (221).[4] Baca points to allusions to passages not only in Book I, the "Cynthia" or "Monobiblos," but in Book

II as well. It is clear that Piccolomini read and digested the text and that these are amatory elegies in the Propertian style.

These two extremes either of casual allusion to Propertius, as in Salutati and Politian, or of large-scale borrowing, as in Piccolomini, are apparent in Italian literature until the nineteenth century.[5] Cristoforo Landino, still in the fifteenth century, shows extensive use, and Ariosto, in his lyrics, alludes to Propertius without making any substantial use of the classical poet (the allusions in the *Orlando Furioso* are much more rich). Marsilio Ficino alludes to our poet, Pontano mentions him, Fulvio Testi wrote poetry influenced by all the Roman elegists, some to a mistress named "Cintia," and Fontana composed a book of *Amori*, also under influence of the elegists. Carducci, in his conception of the underworld, has borrowed from Propertius 4.7, and at the end of the nineteenth century, we find the unusual case of Vincenzo Padula, who wrote a book on Propertius. But we must postpone discussion of Padula, for he belongs to the rather different group of modernists. All of this indicates that after Petrarch, as Duff stated, "since the Renaissance, he [Propertius] has been sure of recognition, though not always of recognition as high as he deserves." This latter recognition did not materialize until the nineteenth century.

The popularity of Propertius among the Italians assured him a certain amount of attention in England once the Renaissance spread there in the sixteenth century. Oddly there seems to have been no early translation of Propertius into English, and indeed the earliest date listed by Harrauer (36) for a complete translation is 1848 (cf. Lathrop 310). The first Latin edition of Propertius printed in England was published, according to Harrauer (18), in 1534, and allusions to Propertius began to appear soon afterwards. Probably some of the first were in Thomas Campion's poems; that poet made great use of Catullus (also in the edition of 1534), as well as of Propertius.[6] One poem that is interesting in its similarity to Petrarch's eclectic mixture of Horace and Propertius in "Ponmi ove 'l sole" is Campion's adaptation of Catullus 5, the famous "Viuamus, mea Lesbia, atque amemus" poem:

My sweetest Lesbia, let us live and love,
And, though the sager sort our deeds reprove,
Let us not way them: heav'ns great lampes doe dive
Into their west, and straite againe revive,
But, soone as once set is our little light,
Then must we sleepe one ever-during night.
If all would lead their lives in love like mee,

Then bloudie swords and armour would not be,
No drum nor trumpet peaceful sleepes should move,
Unles alar'me came from campe of love:
But fooles do live, and wast their little light,
And seek with paine their ever-during night.
When timely death my life and fortune ends,
Let not my hearse be vext with mourning friends,
But let all lovers, rich in triumph, come,
And with sweet pastimes grace my happie tombe;
And, Lesbia, close up though my little light,
And Crowne with love my ever-during night.

(18)

The beginning is clearly a version of Catullus' poem, which in Campion's time was extremely popular; many references are collected by Campion's editor, Davis (18). But the Propertian nature of the rest of the poem was not explored until 1952, when Cunningham showed that the overlap between the idea of impending death in Catullus 5 and the Propertian fascination with the same theme drew Campion into Propertian material. Lines 7–8 are extremely close (Cunningham calls them a "translation") to Propertius 2.15.41 and 43, oddly the same poem imitated by Petrarch:

qualem si cuncti cuperent decurrere uitam . . .
nec ferrum crudele neque esset bellica nauis.

Ah, men are fools who do not pass their life so . . .
Did they, there'd be no need for swords and warships.

(Carrier's translation)

Although the contact between the Catullan and Propertian passages is close, as with Petrarch the omissions are significant. Line 42 of Propertius,

> et pressi multo membra iacere mero,
>
> limbs languorous and heavy with much wine
> (Carrier's translation),

has been omitted by Campion for obvious reasons, and references to current political matters in lines 44–46 have also been removed. It may be, as Cunningham suggests, that line 17 is reminiscent of the last couplet of the Propertian poem (the only real similarities are "includet" and "close up"), but in any case the Campion poem is thoroughly dominated by the Catullan model, and the Propertian material is supplementary. The effect is rather like in the Petrarchan poem discussed above; diverse classical sources are melded together to create an entirely new poetic atmosphere with a richness that can be brought to the poem only by a reader knowledgeable in classical literature, although one can certainly understand the poem without its sources. Still, as with Petrarch, there is little to indicate that Campion really understands Propertius as a poet different from Catullus; this sort of understanding had to wait.

Of the other allusions to Propertius noted by Davis, one in particular will be of interest to classicists. The allusion has been recognized at least since Bullen's edition of Campion in 1903. Davis' text of Campion reads:

> When thou must home to shades of underground,
> And there arriv'd, a newe admired guest,
> The beauteous spirits do ingirt thee round,
> White Iope, blith Hellen, and the rest,
> To heare the stories of thy finisht love,
> From that smoothe toong whose musicke hell can move:
>
> Then wilt thou speake of banqueting delights,
> Of masks and revels which sweete youth did make,
> Of Turnies and great challenges of knights,

And all these triumphes for thy beauties sake:
When thou hast told these honours done to thee,
Then tell, o tell, how thou did'st murther me.

(46)

This should strike all Propertius scholars as an obvious reference to one of the most famous textual *cruces* in Propertius (2.28.49–54):

sunt apud infernos tot milia formosarum:
  pulchra sit in superis, si licet, una locis!
uobiscum est Iope, uobiscum candida Tyro,
  uobiscum Europe nec proba Pasiphae,
et quot Troia tulit uetus et quot Achaia formas,
  et Thebae et Priami diruta regna senis.

there are so many beauties in your kingdom—
may we not keep this girl, our loveliest, here?
Iope's yours—Europa, white-skinned Tyro,
Pasiphae, who bore the Minotaur,
the fairest Greeks, the loveliest of Trojans—
Apollo's Troy, old Priam's, now no more.

(Carrier's translation)

Barber, among other editors, obelizes "Iope," marking textual corruption. This is indeed an important reading and the one that assures us of Propertian imitation in Campion. Iope, or rather the two Iopes,[7] were such rare figures that the later humanist manuscripts altered the text to "Iole," Heracles' wife. In fact there is no need for obelization; Knoche has shown that the dark, Egyptian Iope (also called Cassiope, and the eponym for the city Iope or Joppa) provides a contrast to the beauty of "candida Tyro" ("fair Tyro", 55–56). Campion of course did not know this and transferred the epithet "candida" ("white") to Iope.

Campion's other changes are noteworthy. He has streamlined the passage with the omission of Tyro, Europa, and Pasiphae, and probably borrowed Helen from line 53. The notion of discussing beauty with these women is apparently borrowed from an earlier passage of the poem (ll. 27–28), in which Propertius mentions the possibility of discussing in the underworld with Semele the risk involved in being attractive. More noteworthy is the complete change of situation in the two poems. In Propertius 2.28 Cynthia is ill and in danger of dying, and the speaker begs the gods for improved health. In Campion's poem the speaker has been killed by the woman, although this is not revealed until the last line. But the Propertian allusion still provides a great deal to the poem. Campion evokes the feeling given by many Propertian catalogs of women, a feeling which is derived, through pseudo-Hesiod's *Catalog of Women* (or *Ehoie*), from Odysseus' tour of the underworld in *Odyssey* 9; this tradition, and the Homeric feeling created by Propertius, have been well described by Boyancé ("Properce" 172–93). Campion hence creates a Propertian mood and so again makes use of the classical learning that some readers brought to the poem.

A slightly younger contemporary of Campion, Thomas Carew, was also an admirer of Propertius, and in his poems to Celia he made use of Propertius' poetry; in fact the group about Ben Jonson (Carew, Herrick, Lovelace, Suckling, Howell, Cartright, and Randolph) was profoundly affected by Propertius, although their use of him differed little from their treatment of Tibullus.[8] A more interesting situation arises in the writings of their more celebrated contemporary and leader, Ben Jonson. Jonson's relatively infrequent allusion to Propertius and Tibullus is also documented by McEuen (140–42), who concludes that "though he borrowed seldom from these elegists, his phraseology is sufficiently close to theirs to indicate familiarity with them in the original" (140). Jonson accurately quotes Propertius in *The Masque of Queens* (7: 306) and brings him onstage in the *Poetaster*. Propertius is there described as still sad over Cynthia's decease and appears in act 2, scene 2 as one not feeling well and consequently saying very little; later he is described as hiding at Cynthia's grave. That is indeed the last we hear of him, and he serves more or less as a piece of dramatic scenery rather than as an integral character. More interesting, however, are the four so-called "Propertian elegies" in *The Under-wood*, 38–41. Herford-Simpson-Simpson conclude that since the poems "differ totally in spirit as in quality of poetic fibre from the undoubtedly Jonsonian 'elegy' which follows" and since one of the four poems was also published in Donne's works, the four are by Donne rather than by Jonson (2: 383–84). One reason why this is of interest is that Donne's allusions to Propertius, like Jonson's, are also sparse,[9] although one can see why Propertius would appeal to a metaphysical more than to a neoclassical poet. Propertius' extensive use of imagery would have seemed more effective to Donne than to Jonson.

Let us analyze, then, one of these "Propertian elegies," without becoming entangled in the dispute over authorship. Perhaps 39, also claimed for Donne, is most suitable:

To make the Doubt clear that no Woman's true,
    Was it my fate to prove it full to you?
Thought I, but one had breath'd the purer Ayre
    And must she needs be false, because she's faire?
Is it your beauties Marke, or of your youth,
    or your perfection, not to study truth;
Or think you heaven is deafe? or hath no eyes?
    Or those it has, winke at your perjuries?
Are vowes so cheape with women? or the matter
    Whereof they are made, that they are writ in water;
And blowne away with wind? or doth their breath,
    Both hot and cold at once, threat life and death?
Who could have thought so many accents sweet
    Tun'd to our words, so many sighes should meet
Blowne from our hearts, so many oathes and teares
    Sprinkled among, all sweater by our feares,
And the Divine Impression of stolne kisses,
    That seal'd the rest, could now prove empty blisses?
Did you draw bonds to forfeit? Signe, to breake?
    Or must we read you quite from what you speake,
And find the truth out the wrong way? or must
    He first desire you false, would wish you just?
O, I profane! though most of women be
    The common Monster, Love shall except thee,

My dearest Love, how ever jealousie,
With Circumstance, might urge the contrarie.
Sooner I'll thinke the Sunne would cease to cheare
The teeming Earth, and that forget to beare;
Sooner that Rivers would run back, or Thames
With ribs of Ice in June would bind his streames:
Or Nature, by whose strength the world indures,
Would change her course, before you alter yours:
But, O, that treacherous breast, to whom, weake you,
Did trust our counsells, and we both may rue,
Having his falsehood found too late! 'Twas he
That made me cast you Guiltie, and you me.
Whilst he, black wretch, betray's each simple word
We spake, unto the cunning of a third!
Curst may he be, that so our love hath slaine,
and wander wretched on the earth, as *Cain*,
Wretched as he, and not deserve least pittie;
In plaguing him let miserie be wittie.
Let all eyes shun him, and he shun each eye,
Till he be noysome as his infamie;
May he without remorse deny God thrice,
And not be trusted more on his soules price;
And after all selfe-torment, when he dyes,
May Wolves teare out his heart, Vultures his eyes,
Swyne eat his Bowels, and his falser Tongue,
That utter'd all, be to some Raven flung,
And let his Carrion corse be a longer feast
To the Kings Dogs, then any other beast.
Now I have curst, let us our love revive;
In me the flame was never more alive.
I could begin againe to court and praise,
And in that pleasure lengthen the short dayes
Of my lifes lease; like Painters that doe take
Delight, not in made workes, but whilst they make.
I could renew those times, when first I saw
Love in your eyes, that gave my tongue the Law
To like what you lik'd, and at Masques, or Playes,
Commend the selfe-same Actors, the same wayes;

Aske how you did? and often with intent
Of being officious, grew impertinent;
All of which were such soft pastimes, as in these
Love was as subtly catch'd as a Disease.
But, being got, it is a treasure, sweet,
Which to defend, is harder than to get;
And ought not be profan'd on either part,
For though 'tis got by chance, 'tis kept by art.
(8: 194–97)

We need to ask why Herford-Simpson-Simpson (Jonson 2: 383) refer to the poem and its neighboring poems as "Propertian." The poem is clearly in the tradition of Roman elegy. It includes the standard *topoi* (commonplaces) used by the Roman elegists and by the other poets in Jonson's group, the most obvious of which are the *adynata* (list of impossibilities) in lines 27–33 and the suggestion in lines 10–11 that feminine promises are written on water or wind. Many examples of such themes have been collected by others (McEuen 124–40; Aiken), and no elaboration is required here. But there are other aspects of the poem that are characteristic of Propertius but not of Tibullus or of Ovid in his *Amores*. The emotion is extreme, especially in the rather violent curses of lines 39–52. There is also the self-address and retrospection characteristic of Propertius (ll. 2–18), the use of allusion (here to Cain, l. 40), but especially the rambling nature of the whole poem. The work begins with a suggestion that the mistress has been unfaithful (ll. 1–2), and the poet reflects upon this until line 26, when he has changed his mind and no longer considers her unfaithful. Then come the *adynata* (ll. 27–33), followed by the explanation of the problem—their troubles are due to another party, who until now has not been mentioned. The mistress has without discretion shared their secrets with this man, who then created rumors (ll. 34–38). This new character in the poem then is cursed (ll. 39–52). Suddenly in line 53 the tone changes, as the speaker of the poem calls for love to be renewed, and the poem closes with the speaker's assertion that his love has actually been strengthened by this incident and that he will now work harder to keep his love.

The language of this poem cannot really be called imagist, but it contains the violence of expression and emotion that many critics of more classical taste have censured in Propertius. And this structure, with reversals of emotion and attitude and a constantly changing presentation of ideas, is remarkably like the Propertian structures examined in the preceding chapters and also unlike the usual poetry of Jonson. The unexpected appearance of the confidant in line 33 is a good example of Propertian style, as is the firm reaffirmation of love at the end of the poem in the face of apparent infidelity. (This style is probably a better reason for questioning Jonson's authorship than the implicit attitude toward women that Herford-Simpson-Simpson offer as evidence of Jonson's spurious authorship.) When compared to Petrarch's and Campion's use of Propertius, this poem is indeed unusual. Petrarch employs Propertius because he is creating what we now call the Petrarchan tradition, where the poet associates himself faithfully with his mistress in the Catullan elegiac tradition. But poems such as "Ponmi ove 'l sole" read more like Horace than Propertius, and the Propertian allusion there is in fact adapted to a Horatian situation. Campion's allusions to Propertius are more Catullan and read like the adaptation of Propertian phrases to poems of the Catullan variety. But the writer of this poem, whether Jonson, Donne, or someone else, revives the style of Propertius. He may, in fact, be the first writer in more than twelve centuries really to have understood Propertius, the first to perceive the aims of Propertian language and structure.

Viewed in historical terms, this situation makes perfect sense. Propertius reacts against classical language and structure, creating instead images linked in an associative manner. The high Renaissance, whether in Italy or in England, represents an attempt to revive the classical ideals against which Propertius reacted. This is especially true of a neoclassicist like Jonson, who is far more oriented toward Horace and the more standard authors.

Jonson's contemporaries were exposed to Propertius, at least in some derivative form, but they read him as though he were Tibullus or Ovid and consequently allude to his themes and even to passages, but without really seeing what he represented. The same is true of Milton, whose Latin poems contain references to and virtual quotations of Propertius (a list is given in Milton 380), but who, in his more classical and Vergilian orientation, does not write truly Propertian material.

There is, then, an almost direct correlation between the classicism of an age and its ability to understand Propertius. This might help to explain his virtual absence from eighteenth-century England. It is only in the later nineteenth century, when, through the post-Renaissance efforts of Locke, Darwin, Nietzsche, and others, confidence in reason has been shaken, that poetry such as Propertius' can come back into fashion. His return can be seen in three quite different authors in quite different movements in different countries.

The first revival of Propertius in the late nineteenth century is also the most obscure. The Italian scholar-priest-radical Vincenzo Padula wrote in 1871 a treatise entitled *Pauca Quae in Sexto Aurelio Propertio Vincentius Padula ab Acrio Animadvertebat* (*A Few Things on Sextus Aurelius Propertius which Vincenzo Padula from Acrio Noticed*). Until very recently the treatise has been unavailable and even unpublished, but fortunately it has now been edited and translated into English by Tomaszuk, and information on this work has been provided by Scafoglio (15, 21 nn. 56–57, 58, 68, 107; cf. Muscetta 8: 1, 282; Sullivan, *Propertius* 50). The treatise attempted to reinterpret Propertius and his love in terms of Italian events, especially as seen by a southern Italian. Padula was involved in the movement for Italian nationalism and saw in Propertius a precursor of this attitude. In a letter of 9 November 1871, he expressed his intentions as follows: "To reinterpret the Italian verses, to make them modern, to make them Italian, to make them useful for those of us who write prose and verse: there is the concept which has guided me in the present work" (Scafoglio 28, cf. 21 n. 57).[10] In her introduction to Padula's book, Tomaszuk compares this to the later use made of Propertius by Pound (11), and the similarity is striking. Tomaszuk is taken by the "modern" appearance of many of Padula's ideas. He perceived the relation between mythology and pictorial art as a substitution by Propertius for Tibullus' more pastoral setting:

> Therefore the critics have no reason to criticize the myths to which Propertius frequently alludes because they are not foreign, incongruous, dragged-in, but a vital part of his theme; for if Cynthia had lived in the country, the poet would certainly have borrowed his imagery from country life; but since she lived in Rome, it was right that the poems written in her honour should be sprinkled with those myths which could be seen everywhere in Rome, sculptured or painted, and that they should give preference to Rome in her greatness. (Tomaszuk's translation, 96)

Padula also anticipates the structural arguments presented in chapter 2: "Moreover, much of the obscurity is due to the fact that Propertius, swept away by the tide of his passions, jumps very quickly from one idea to another; and since those passions are so real and so vividly expressed, can the reader help exclaiming: Is it not Erato who is singing?" (Tomaszuk's translation, 99).[11] Padula also comments on the translation of Propertius into Italian, especially with regard to Fulvio Testi (101) and Tasso (106–9).

Tomaszuk's comparison of Padula to Pound provokes thought, but the scholarly reaction to Padula makes a striking contrast to that which followed Pound's *Homage to Sextus Propertius*. Padula was ignored for many years, until Benedetto Croce took an interest in his ideas. In chapter 3 I discussed the controversy between Croce, on the one hand, and the classicists Jachmann and Pasquali, on the other, over the text and interpretation of Propertius 2.15. Also on the issue of the value of Padula's ideas Croce was assailed by Pasquali, although more recent classicists such as Tomaszuk have reacted more favorably (Croce, *Poesia* 72–96; Pasquali 46–47; cf. La Penna, *L'integrazione* 300–313; Scafoglio 58, 68). Certainly Croce, like Padula and Pound, although not a classicist and perhaps because he was not a classicist, was able to transcend the narrow limits of classical scholarship and to suggest new modes of interpretation that have made Propertius more relevant to the twentieth century.

A short time after Padula, Propertius played a role in the decadence movement. Evans refers to the movement, involving Pater, Wilde, Beardsley, and Dowson, in the following terms: "Even more precisely than with Swinburne the indebtedness was to French verse, particularly to Verlaine, modified by the Latin influence of the Latin lyric of Horace and Propertius" (184). Dowson indeed put Propertius to good use. Most often pointed to is his fascinating poem, "Non Sum Qualis Eram Bonae Sub Regno Cynarae," which borrows its title from Horace:

Last night, ah yesternight, betwixt her lips and mine
There fell thy shadow, Cynara! thy breath was shed
Upon my soul between the kisses and the wine;
And I was desolate and sick of an old passion,
    Yea, I was desolate and bowed my head:
I have been faithful to thee, Cynara! in my fashion.

All night upon mine heart I felt her warm heart beat,
Night-long within mine arms in love and sleep she lay;
Surely the kisses of her bought red mouth were sweet;
But I was desolate and sick of an old passion
    When I awoke and found the dawn was grey:
I have been faithful to thee, Cynara! in my fashion.

I have forgot much, Cynara! gone with the wind,
Flung roses, roses riotously with the throng,
Dancing, to put thy pale, lost lilies out of mind;
But I was desolate and sick of an old passion,
    Yea, all the time, because the dance was long:
I have been faithful to thee, Cynara! in my fashion.

I cried for madder music and for stronger wine,
But when the feast is finished and the lamps expire,
Then falls thy shadow, Cynara! the night is thine;
And I am desolate and sick of an old passion,
    Yea hungry for the lips of my desire:
I have been faithful to thee, Cynara! in my fashion.

(*Poems* 58)

This poem, which appeared in 1891, is generally considered Dowson's best, even perhaps by Dowson.[12] But much of the discussion of the poem has focused upon the identity of "Cynara." Dowson's friend Arthur Symons was perhaps the first to recognize the poem's importance: "In the lyric in which he has epitomized himself and his whole life, a lyric which is certainly one of the greatest lyrical poems of our time . . . he has for once said everything, and he has said it to an intoxicating and perhaps immortal music" (qtd. in Swann 45). But Plarr, another friend, steered the interpretation in the direction of Propertius: "Ernest Dowson loved his Propertius. . . . There is a singular, a poignant parallelism between the great and prolonged *cri du coeur* of the old Roman and the modern's sorrowful lament, as expressed, for instance, in his Cynara poem, . . . the boldness of which [is] august with the spirit of antiquity, as though the pagan had passed into and inspired the unhappy lad of the day before yesterday." A note adds that although the title of the poem is from Horace, and perhaps Cynara from Horace's Cinara, "Horace suggested, but Propertius inspired" (*Ernest Dowson* 57). Aside from reminiscences of Propertian poems, as for example to Propertius 4.8.43–48, where in the absence of Cynthia Propertius cannot enjoy the company of the courtesans Phyllis and Teia (including the throwing of roses), there is very much a Propertian atmosphere in the poem. In the emotional devotion to a mistress, especially when with others, and in the passionate devotion to a lost, unregainable experience, we find the Propertian way of life. There is a haunting, almost macabre, feeling about this poem, which some would attribute to Dowson's role in the decadence movement, but it is a decadence which derives from Roman poetry and especially from Propertius.

According to Plarr, one of the reasons for Dowson's admiration for Propertius is that he was attempting, in his own poetry, to duplicate "Latin brevity and clarity" (*Ernest Dowson* 59). That same motivation is apparently at least part of what led Ezra Pound to imagism and, ultimately, to Propertius. With the appearance in 1917 of the *Homage to Sextus Propertius*, our Roman elegist finally emerges into the literary mainstream. A great deal has been written about Pound and Propertius (Forbes; Sullivan, *Pound*, "Homage," "Translator"; Feder 92–99, 120 n. 72; Pasoli 112–14), and extended treatment need not be given here. Pound's original audience was not greatly impressed. This is clear not only from the sources gathered by Sullivan, but especially from the article of Forbes written shortly after World War II. Almost as stringent as Forbes' criticism, as can be seen from the title, was that written by the scholar-author Robert Graves entitled "Dr. Syntax and Mr. Pound." (Pound never completed his Ph.D. and was never really accepted by the academic community.) Graves blends parts of Pound's eulogy in *The Times Literary Supplement* into a fictitious scene from a British "fourth form" classroom. Oddly Pound and A. E. Housman wrote little about each other and nothing about the other's work on Propertius. Housman may have thought that Pound's parodic and mocking poem of 1911, "Mr. Housman's Message" (*Personae* 43, originally in *Canzioni*) and his vigorous blast in 1934 at Housman's ideas on literary criticism ("Housman") were unworthy of reply—perhaps even unworthy of reading. Naturally Pound's political and mental problems did not help his reputation, but what most offended classicists were the blatant errors in translation. The misspelled classical names, for instance, were easy targets. Sullivan, with Pound's permission, corrected some of these in his newly edited text, but others were done by Pound for metrical reasons, and he would not allow them to be corrected. The simple fact is that Pound was not greatly concerned about such details of classical scholarship and was interested in something quite different. Sullivan has called his interest "creative translation," using the phrase in the subtitle of his study of the *Homage* (*Pound*). Pound wanted to generate, for the English-reading audience, an experience something like that of a first-century B.C. Roman reading Propertius. Consequently the language is modernized and colloquialized, and Propertius reads rather like a Pound. Sullivan has suggested several reasons for Pound's affinity to Propertius, namely his belief that Propertius' political and literary milieus were similar to his own and that

Propertius had engaged in what Pound called *logopoeia.* The present study has attempted to suggest another—Propertius' poetry is imagist in tenor. His poems progress, in associational fashion, from image to image, and do not follow the standard classical and rational patterns. Two of the poems analyzed in chapter 4, in fact, employ the technique that Pound called superposition, in which narrative is superimposed upon image or vice versa.

In light of the modernist in Propertius, it would be surprising if James Joyce was not influenced in some way by our classical poet, although I am aware of no study in this connection. Still, it seems to me that Joyce had Propertius in mind when he wrote the famous description of Stephen's dream about his mother: "Silently, in a dream she had come to him after her death, her wasted body within its loose brown grave-clothes giving off an odour of wax and rosewood, her breath, that had bent upon him, mute, reproachful, a faint odour of wetted ashes" (*Ulysses* 5). She reproaches Stephen for not praying for her on her deathbed. In Propertius 4.7 the ghost of Cynthia appears to the speaker in a dream and complains about his failure, among other things, to pray at her funeral. Propertius describes Cynthia's "grave-clothes," also charred by ashes. The Propertian dream, like the entire *Ulysses*, is built upon a Homeric model, as many scholars have observed (Benediktson, "'Elegiacization'" 21–22). Furthermore this famous poem was also imitated by Carducci and studied by Padula and Croce (the latter after the publication of *Ulysses*), and hence might well have been easily accessible to Joyce.

Pound's Latin was not nearly so good as Dowson's, but his contribution has been much greater. Sullivan rightly suggests that the *Homage* revolutionized the practice of translation in the twentieth century. As an example he discusses Robert Lowell's "The Ghost," a "creative translation" of Propertius 4.7. But after Sullivan's publication of *Ezra Pound and Sextus Propertius*, Lowell translated another poem of Propertius, 4.3, which Lowell called "Arethusa to Lycotas." Propertius' lines and Lowell's translation, to which I have added line numbers, follow:

Haec Arethusa suo mittit mandata Lycotae
  cum totiens absis, si potes esse meus.
si qua tamen tibi lecturo pars oblita desit,
  haec erit e lacrimis facta litura meis;
aut si qua incerto fallet te littera tractu,
  signa meae dextrae iam morientis erunt.
te modo uiderunt iteratos Bactra per ortus,
  te modo munito Sericus hostis equo,
hibernique Getae, pictoque Britannia curru,
  ustus et Eoa decolor Indus aqua.
haecne marita fides et †parce auia noctes†,
  cum rudis urgenti bracchia uicta dedi?
quae mihi deductae fax omen praetulit, illa
  traxit ab euerso lumina nigra rogo;
et Stygio sum sparsa lacu, nec recta capillis,
  uitta data est: nupsi non comitante deo.
omnibus heu portis pendent mea noxia uota:
  texitur haec castris quarta lacerna tuis.
occidat, immerita qui carpsit ab arbore uallum
  et struxit querulas rauca per ossa tubas,
dignior obliquo funem qui torqueat Ocno,
  aeternusque tuam pascat, aselle, famem!
dic mihi, num teneros urit lorica lacertos,
  num grauis imbellis atterit hasta manus.
haec noceant potius, quam dentibus ulla puella
  det mihi plorandas per tua colla notas!
diceris et macie uultum tenuasse: sed opto
  e desiderio sit color iste meo.
at mihi cum noctes induxit uesper amaras,
  si qua relicta iacent, osculor arma tua.
tum queror in toto non sidere pallia lecto,
  lucis et auctores non dare carmen auis.
noctibus hibernis castrensia pensa laboro
  et Tyria in clauos uellera secta tuos;
et disco, qua parte fluat uincendus Araxes,
  quot sine aqua Parthus milia currat equus,
cogor et e tabula pictos ediscere mundos,
  qualis et haec docti sit positura dei,

quae tellus sit lenta gelu, quae putris ab aestu,
uentus in Italiam qui bene uela ferat.
assidet una soror curis et pallida nutrix
peierat hiberni temporis esse moras.
felix Hippolyte! nuda tulit arma papilla
et texit galea barbara molle caput.
Romanis utinam patuissent castra puellis!
essem militiae sarcina fida tuae,
nec me tardarent Scythia iuga, cum pater altas
†Africus† in glaciem frigore nectit aquas.
omnis amor magnus, sed aperto in coniuge maior:
hanc Venus, ut uiuat, uentilat ipsa facem.
nam mihi quo Poenis ter purpura fulgeat ostris
chrystallusque meas ornet aquosa manus?
omnia surda tacent, rarisque assueta Kalendis
uix aperit clausos una puella Lares,
Craugidos et catulae uox est mihi grata querentis:
illa tui partem uindicat una tori.
flore sacella tego, uirbenis compita uelo,
et crepat ad ueteres herba Sabina focos.
siue in finitimo gemuit stans noctua tigno,
seu uoluit tangi parca lucerna mero,
illa dies hornis caedem denuntiat agnis,
succinctique calent ad noua lucra popae.
ne, precor, ascensis tanti sit gloria Bactris,
raptaue odorato carbasa lina duci,
plumbea cum tortae sparguntur pondere fundae
subdolus et uersis increpat arcus equis!
sed (tua sic domitis Parthae telluris alumnis
pura triumphantis hasta sequatur equos)
incorrupta mei conserua foedera lecti!
hac ego te sola lege redisse uelim;
armaque cum tulero portae uotiua Capenae,
subscribam: 'SALVO GRATA PUELLA VIRO.'

Arethusa to Lycotas
(Propertius, Book IV, 3)
Arethusa sends her Lycotas this command:

if I can call you, always absent, mine,
if some letters have an uncertain outline,
they're proofs I write you with a dying hand.
Bactra twice visited, you rushed to see

the taunting Neurican on his armored horse,
the wintry Getae, Britain's painted cars,
the sunburnt Hindo by his sultry sea.
Is this our marriage? Hymen was gone when I

a stranger to love, and afraid of freedom, chose
the ominous torch that lit me to your house—
the coronet on my hair was set awry.
May whoever cut tentstakes from the harmless ash,

or carved the hoarse-complaining trumpet from bone—
die worse than Ocnus, who sits aslant to twine
his rope in hell forever to feed the ass.
Does the breastplate bruise your soft white flesh,

are your civil hands blistered by the war spear?
Better these hurt you than some girl should scar
your neck with toothmarks for my tears to heal.
Now sharper nights attend the evening star,

the blanket will not stay put on my bed—
I could kiss your dull weapons you left here dead . . .
the birds, that herald morning, sing no more.
I know the painted world of maps, I know

which way the Araxes you will ford must flow,
how far without water a Parthian horse will fly—
I've placed your almost polar city, Dai.
I know which lands the sun hurts, which the frost—

which wind will blow you home to Italy.
My older sister and old nurse swear to me
it's only the heavy winter holds you fast.
Hippolyta was lucky, she could enter the ring

barebreasted; a captain's helmet hid her curls.
I wish our Roman camps admitted girls,
I'd be faithful baggage for your soldiering.
Mountains would not frighten me with height,

or Jupiter chaining the high streams with ice.
All love is great—a wife has greater love,
Venus blows on this flame that it may live.
All's dead here—at rare Kalends, a lonely housemaid

opens the Lares on her perfunctory round;
I wait for the whine of Craugus, the small hound;
he is only claiming your place in my bed.
If the barn-owl scream from the neighboring oak,

or wine is sprinkled on the sputtering lamps,
that day requires we kill the first-year lambs;
blackmail hurries the stately priest to work.
I've no cause to shine in bridal attire,

make chrystals glitter like waterdrops on my ears;
I hang shrines with flowers, the crossroad with green firs;
marjoram crackles in the ancestral fire;
Is glory taking Bactra's walls by force,

or tearing the turban from a perfumed king,
while the bow twangs from their hypocrite flying horse,
and lead scatters like hailstones from the twisted sling?
When their young men are gone, and slavery heals

their widows, and the spear without a head
drags at our triumphant horse's heels—
remember the vow that binds you to our bed.
If you come back to me by day or night,

and make us for the moment man and wife,
I'll bring your arms to the Capua Gate, and write:
From a girl grateful for her husband's life.

(136–38, Lowell's italics)

Day by Day appeared in 1975, and so this poem brings us almost to the present day. The poem ends the book in which it appears and fittingly echoes the book's first poem "Ulysses and Circe" (Fein 175). Perhaps the most striking aspect of the poem to a classicist is its brevity. Anyone who has put Greek or Latin into English knows that the translation produced is generally longer than the original. We shall see how Lowell does this. Also striking to the classicist is the elimination of the elegiac couplet. To Propertius' audience meter and genre were almost synonymous, but not so to Lowell's audience, who can read the poem in this form and still call it "elegy" (insofar as it is important to the modern audience even to give a generic label to a literary work). The formal unit here is the stanza, and these stanzas are reinforced by a rhyme scheme which varies and even disappears occasionally, although syntactically each stanza is tied to its predecessor. (Some of course have found stanzaic composition in Propertius, but Lowell's stanzas do not correspond to any such in Propertius.) But the frequent end-stops for most lines in Lowell's version add an effect something like that obtained by the elegiac couplet. Since there is not room here to analyze the entire poem in detail, I shall examine Propertius' lines 1–10, which in Lowell become lines 1–8.

Most obviously, Lowell made many minor changes of syntax. In line 1 there is the relatively slight change of plural to singular in "haec mandata" to "this command." In line 2 the *cum* clause has become a participle, and "potes esse meus" ("you can be mine") has become, with relatively little change in meaning, "I can call." Lines 3–4 of Propertius are simply omitted, presumably because their meaning is repeated somewhat in lines 5–6, and so the sense unit of Propertius, lines 1–6 has become Lowell, lines 1–4. Propertius, lines 5–6 are only slightly modified; the "you" is transferred from line 5 to line 4, and we lose the insignificant detail that Arethusa is right-handed. Propertius' line 7 has become merely two words in line 5 and involves a controversial reading of these lines (see, e.g., Richardson). The next line (Propertius, l. 8; Lowell, l. 6) involves a change which is only comprehensible to a classicist. "Sericus" has been translated as "Neurican." Evidently whatever text Lowell used contained Jacob's emendation "Neuricus" ("Sericus" is an emendation of Beroaldus; most manuscripts read "hericus"). There is also in these lines a change of the direct object "te" ("you") to become the active subject of these lines. Finally, in Lowell's line 8 the word "sultry," borrowed perhaps from "ustus" (which Lowell translates as "sunburnt") replaces "Eoa," which simply means "eastern."

This list of details could be enlarged and the analysis could be extended to the rest of the poem, but it should be clear how Lowell shortens the poem and our time would be better spent assessing the product. In spite of the changes, we have here a remarkably Propertian poem. There is the Propertian linguistic conciseness and syntactic distortion, although this is perhaps more visible in the frequent dashes throughout the poem. Lowell conveys very well in his second stanza the catalog of exotic names and omits those items which an English reader would find offensive, most notably the parallel syntactic structures—"si qua . . . si qua"; "te modo . . . te modo"; "-que . . . -que . . . et") ("if any . . . if any"; "you now . . . you now"; "and . . . and . . . and". The result is a Propertian poem, but actually a Propertian-like experience for the non-Latinist.

What I have described here, of course, is also the attempt of Pound as described by Sullivan. And there is much of the Poundian in this poem, which illustrates how thoroughly Pound has influenced the practice of literary translation in the twentieth century. But un-Poundian is Lowell's faithfulness to Latin scholarship. One does not, as with Pound, ever have the feeling that Lowell does not understand the Latin or has not troubled to consult his dictionaries or commentaries (and although commentaries on Propertius in English are much more accessible now than in 1917, Pound still had access to Butler's English commentary of 1905 [*Opera*]). I might note one small error: the dog "Craugis" in line 55 (Lowell, l. 43) has been changed to "Craugus." No one would seriously object to this except poor Craugis, whose gender has been changed from feminine to masculine. Lowell might have been fooled by the Greek genitive (although Lowell of course had also translated Greek texts into English), and at any rate the word, like many proper names, is missing from the standard dictionaries, perhaps because of its spelling difficulties as preserved in the manuscripts. And "illa" ("she") in the next line, referring to Craugis, has been translated as "he," so evidently the change of gender is intentional. Lowell has also taken "dei" ("of a god") in line 38 as a place ("city, Dai" in his line 28); it may have been capitalized in his Latin text and in any case is confusing Latin. But in general Lowell has avoided the type of faults criticized in Pound, and we find here a very effective "creative translation" of Propertius.

Perhaps the way to end this brief and, by necessity, incomplete study of Propertius' influence is to return to A. E. Housman. One would suspect that Housman could not have worked as extensively with Propertius as he did and not have been uninfluenced in his own poetry. Norman Marlow has studied Housman's sources in detail, and concludes his discussion with a treatment of Propertius (39–41). Marlow finds that "Propertius' preoccupation with love and death leads him on occasion to neurotic excesses of fulsomeness or vituperation, but often he rises above his self-centredness and writes in the high Roman fashion of love and the grave. It is here that his influence upon Housman is evident. . . . It is the youthful intensity of Propertius and his preoccupation with unrequited love that make his atmosphere so like that of *A Shropshire Lad*" (39, 41). Something of this spirit can be seen in the short poem XVI of *A Shropshire Lad* (parodied, incidentally, in Pound's "Mr. Housman's Message"):

> It nods and curtseys and recovers
>   When the wind blows above
> The nettle on the graves of lovers
>   That hanged themselves for love.
>
> The nettle nods, the wind blows over,
>   The man, he does not move,
> The lover of the grave, the lover
>   That hanged himself for love.
>
> (*Poems* 29)

One can see why the young Housman, as a college student at Oxford, was so taken by Propertius. The poem exhibits the morbid and visual association of love with death found so often in Propertius, an association that has formed the subject of Papanghelis' recent study of Propertius.

It seems clear that, until recently, Propertius has been little understood. The Renaissance poets like Petrarch, Campion, and the followers of Jonson understood him not as the anticlassicist he was, but as a standard love poet in the mold of Catullus and Tibullus. Only the elegies written by Jonson (or Donne, or whomever) in any way duplicate the Propertian style. In the ensuing age of classicism again Propertius lost influence, only to regain importance at the end of the nineteenth century. Classicists might disapprove (and have disapproved) of the uses of Propertius by Padula, Dowson, and Pound, but these writers made him available to modern poets and scholars.

In Lowell we have seen the continuing influence not only of Propertius but also of Pound. In Propertius' imagistic style, in his fascination with visual and musical forms and with the psychology of emotions, we find an ancient poet who is truly suited to the twentieth century. His influence is likely to grow, just as interest in him has increased over the past twenty years. Pound may have created new interest in him, but Propertius can now survive on his own.

Notes

Bibliography

Index

Notes

Chapter 1

1. Bailey, "Experiments" 9–20, presents an excellent (and moderate) treatment of the history and problems of Propertian criticism.

2. On Housman's early career see Gow 6–14; Butrica, *Manuscript* 6–7.

3. I have edited all the Latin works that I quote from throughout this book, basing my quotations on the editions listed in the Bibliography.

4. Cf. Stahl 319–20.

5. Cf. Godolphin; Williams, *Tradition* 479; Tränkle 146–47 n. 1.

6. Besides the edition see Richmond, "Archetype," "Reconstruction."

7. See, e.g., Sabbadini; Jachmann 193–228.

8. Sullivan's book also contains Pound's text and Müller's Latin Propertius. See also Sullivan, "Classics."

9. See also Thomas; Yardley. On the "blending of genres" see Kroll. The standard introduction to Roman elegy is still Luck; see also Sullivan, *Essays* for an antiautobiographical approach.

10. On the organization of Book I see Skutsch, "Structure," and for an excellent ring-compositional analysis of an individual poem, Suits. A more general presence of the technique in Propertius has been recognized by Williams, *Figures* 98–102; Nethercut 1820–21, 1826, 1828–30; Stahl 165, 219–29, 231, 286, 303. Among the first observers was Bailey, "Experiments" 18.

11. On the origin, the Homeric use, and ancient critics' knowledge of ring-composition, see Bassett 119–28, 251–52; Whitman 87–101, 249–84, 331–33, 350–53, and pull-out diagram.

12. For a sample breakdown see Fordyce 344. On ring-composition as a Hellenistic device elaborated by Catullus, see Fedeli 24.

Chapter 2

1. Commentary on the poems of Catullus is in Quinn, *Catullus*; detailed but incomplete is Fordyce. Commentary on *Amores*, Book One, is in Barsby.

2. On this ending see Parker, although this poem is not treated. There are good comments on the poem, and on Ovid in general, in Williams, *Tradition* 512–13. An interpretation similar to mine but with different emphasis is in Luck 160–65.

3. See also La Penna, *L'integrazione* 65, who, like Fantazzi 181, thinks Cornelius Gallus should also be considered here.

4. Compare, however, to mine the analysis of Williams, *Figures* 82–84, who sees the poem as unified by the theme of marriage.

5. See Rothstein and, on Phryne, Volkmann qtd. in Ziegler-Sontheimer 4: 826.

6. See Reitzenstein 216, 220; Reitzenstein and Williams (see n. 4) almost alone show an appropriate understanding and appreciation for this poem; ring-composition is found by Rothstein 246.

7. This interpretation of "his . . . uitiis" originates with Reitzenstein 217 and Schöne 17–18 and is now standard; see, e.g., Enk; La Penna, *Properzio* 48. See Enk on ll. 27–34 on pictorial art and on the subject of Paris and Helen, and also Rothstein on l. 15.

8. The passage is also, as will be seen, a good example of Propertius' tendency (demonstrated by Williams, *Figures*) to use myths to develop unexpressed ideas, although Williams' discussion of this passage (87) is rather cursory.

9. Others have argued this; cf. Enk; Butler-Barber.

10. An excellent analysis of the passage and the poem in general is in Reitzenstein 196–203. Stahl 172–88, 348–54 argues for unity based on the use of Lynceus as "foil" to Vergil. Both scholars suggest ring-composition, as I shall also.

11. Bailey, *Propertiana*, removes Heracles from the second couplet. The interpretation here is rejected by Butler, *Opera*. Maass (in Wimmel 206) believed that ll. 33–38 all refer to works by Callimachus and Philetas; an analysis similar to mine is offered by Schöne 15. Stahl 175, 348 sees ll. 33–38 as elegiac material and ll. 39–46 as nonelegiac.

12. Stahl 176–77 sees the tie between ll. 27–35 and 51–54. That ll. 29–30 refer to Aeschylus is argued, for example, by Butler-Barber and Herrmann 141.

13. On the grammar cf. Rothstein. See also Camps and his postscript on 2.34 (2: 235); Schöne 15–16.

14. Stahl 179–81, 183, 352 sees the whole Vergilian passage as critical; Stahl reviews the scholarship, but see also Vessey 65; Carter 42–43; Lefèvre, "Properce" 128–29. Buffa 191–92 steers a middle course.

15. This was suggested to me by Nethercut. Stahl 180, 352 notes the probable reference to *Aeneid* 1.44–45. Carrier, in her translation, takes "nescio quid maius nascitur Iliade" to refer to the pastoral material which follows in ll. 67–76, but most scholars agree that it refers to the *Aeneid*. An anonymous referee called my attention to this and to *Aeneid* 7.45, "maius opus."

16. Wimmel 207 suggests that the wandering style, at least from ll. 46–55, is due to Vergilian imitation.

17. Pioneers in the application of stream-of-consciousness theory include Reitzenstein; Tränkle, especially 143–49; Quinn, *Explorations* 130–97; Sullivan, *Pound*; Tomaszuk. Contemporary or subsequent applications include Pasoli; La Penna, *L'integrazione* 29–30, 64–66; Warden, especially 85–111, 135–39. Lefèvre's quotations ("Properziana" 28) are: "lo scambio di apostrofe," "il carattere fitizio della situazione esterna," "l'incoerenza del tempo rappresentato," "il carattere associativo del concatamento."

Chapter 3

1. King only once (273) uses the term leitmotif.

2. Williams, *Figures* 105, 163–64 emphasizes the repetition of "dies" in ll. 24, 26 and the unity of ll. 42–54 through the references to wine as symbol of love.

3. On Jachmann's influence see Rudd 152 n. 1; for criticisms of Jachmann see Bailey, "Experiments" 12–16.

Chapter 4

1. See especially King, "Studies" 125–46, 199–202; Rothstein 73–74; Curran; Boucher 243; Allen, "Sunt Qui" 130–34; Lyne; the commentaries of Richardson and Hodge-Buttimore. See also Herzberg in Schöne 18; Harmon, "Myth." For bibliography to 1958 see Lieberg, "L'elegia" 308–21, supplemented by Harrauer 44.

2. "Ainsi d'images en images se déroule le récit de cet incident." Besides the works in n. 1 see especially Keyssner 270–74; Dilthey; Helbig 119; Otto, "Particula Prior" 16; Bartholomé 42–44, 64 n. 160; Stoll in Roscher 1: 1, 544–46. See also Rothstein on ll. 7, 19, 23, and 25, and Richardson on ll. 1–5, 20.

3. I follow here the argument and examples of Miner.

4. For the passages see his general index, "Propertius, avoidance of purely visual imagery."

5. "superposition"; "variante picturale"; "C'est l'imagination visuelle de poète qui constitute la lien intérieur de ce development."

6. "visioni," "pericolo," "carattere associativo"; Lefèvre, *Ludibundus* 38–47; Williams, *Figures* 129–31. For bibliography on division, see Wiggers 121 n. 2. Wiggers and Macleod also defend unity. See also Baker, "*Laus*" 684–88, and for a favorable view of the "dream" ("sogno") in ll. 21–58, La Penna, *Properzio* 66. On ll. 1–20 see especially Quinn, *Explorations* 187–97; La Penna, *Properzio* 12–13.

7. "einer Reihe von Bildern"; "Phantasie."

Chapter 5

1. See, e.g., Kenney, *Lucretius* 33–37, with further references; of these see especially Townend.

2. "croyant à la valeur des arts, à celle de l'amour comme forme de vie." See also Alfonsi 28, 31; Veremans.

3. On Epicureanism and pastoral see Walker 22–24, on the lack of pastoral in Propertius Harrington; Krókowsky. On the pastoral Tibullus see Fedeli 36–37; Bright 4–15. On the blending of genres see Kroll; Muecke; Fantazzi 171–91; Krókowsky 180–85.

4. On Messala see Kroll 206, for Vergil and Gallus Muecke 7.8–7.13; Fantazzi 181; Ross.

5. On the city and Epicureanism in Propertius cf. Alfonsi, 63. King, "Studies" 285, 293–94 finds "urban pastoral" in Book I. Something

similar to the concept of poetic retreat developed here can be seen in the analyses of English literature in Martz.

6. Good introductions to Philodemus are in Grube 193–99; Wilkinson; Atkins 2: 47–56.

7. Ὅ γε Νεοπτόλεμος οὐκ ὀρθῶς ἔδοξε τὴν σύνθεσιν τῆς λέξεως τῶν διανοημάτων χωρίζειν (Jensen 10.33–9.2). See also the dissertation summary of Greenberg, "Poetic."

8. For a summary of theories of imitation (other than Philodemus'), see McKeon.

9. For similar passages in *On Poems* see Grube 196–97; on imitation of prior authors see the discussion and references in Grube.

10. Τίς δ'ἀνάγκη τὸ πραττόμενον ἐναργῶς καὶ συντόμως ἀπαγγέλλεσθαι, πολλῶν οὐ μόνον ψευδῶν, ἀλλὰ καὶ μυθωδεστάτων ἐναργέστατα παρὰ τοῖς ποιηταῖς ἀπαγγελλομένων (Jensen 4.6–13); see also Wilkinson 150. On this concept and Epicureanism, see Papanghelis 207–10.

11. See, e.g., Rostagni. On Crocean imagism and intuition see Orsini 24–63, 319–29.

12. On the doctrine see Lee; see also Brink on ll. 151–63 of Horace's *Ars Poetica* and Lucas 258–72 on Aristotle's *Poetics*.

13. See Friedman 103–4; Gifford-Seidman on the *Ulysses* passage (index, "Lessing, Gotthold Ephraim").

Chapter 6

1. There is a treatment of Propertius' influence in Sullivan, *Propertius* 46–53; La Penna, *L'integrazione* 250–99, has a detailed discussion, primarily of his influence on continental writers and scholars.

2. The Wickam-Garrod text is identical to Muscetta's.

3. "E si veda ancora come del verso properziana sia eluso nella traduzione il pronome personale ("huius") per indicare che non solo amorosa é la passione e la vocazione dell'animo."

4. Cf. Paparelli. Analogous perhaps to the case of Piccolomini is the *Elegiae* of Joannes Secundus; see Endres-Gold. On Politian see Muscetta 3: 2, 160 (comparing *Elegia* 5.14 and Propertius 1.18.2).

5. For further references to figures mentioned here see Muscetta's indexes to volumes 4: 1 (Ariosto); 5: 1 (Testi); 6: 1 (Fontana); 8: 1 (Padula). On Landino see Robathan; on Ariosto see also Romizi 23–30; on Ficino

see Lieberg, "Mythologie" 346–47; on Pontano see del Ton; on Carducci see Baldi.

6. Many are noted by Davis, ed. *Campion*—see, e.g., 18, 28, 34, 46nn. See also Aiken 43–44. Better claim as the first allusion may be to Spenser's *Prothalamion*; see West.

7. For more information on Iope see Boucher 259–60, following Boyancé, "Properce" 185–88, 191; Tümpel in Roscher 2: 1, 293–95 (cf. Stoll's addendum); Butler-Barber; Rothstein; Camps; Richardson; Alfonsi 22.

8. For a list of poems by Carew with allusions, see Sadler 150 n. 17; the Propertian sources can be found in the commentary to these poems in the edition of Dunlap, ed. *Carew*; see also Aiken 44–46. On the whole group see McEuen 124–40.

9. There are a few references to Donne in Aiken and no ties of Donne to Propertius.

10. "Ringiovanire i latini versi, farli moderni, farli italiani, farli utili a noi che scriviamo prose e versi: ecco il concetto che mi ha guidato nel presente lavoro."

11. Reitzenstein uses a similar argument to justify Propertian style.

12. On the poem's esteem and "genesis" see Longaker, ed. *Poems* 81–85, including biographical comments; on Dowson's own view see the commentary on the poem in Longaker, ed. *Poems* 207. Papanghelis (54, 209–10) discusses Propertius' influence on Dowson in this and other poems.

Bibliography

Texts, Translations, and Commentaries

Texts and translations of classical authors and commentaries on them are listed by editor's name, while editions of modern authors are listed by author's name. I have edited the Latin texts of Propertius quoted in the text and notes myself, basing the text on Barber but also consulting the editions listed here. The same is true of Ovid and Catullus, based on Kenney and Thomson, respectively. Passing references to classical authors (Demosthenes, *De Corona*; Dio Chrysostom, *Orationes*; Horace, *Ars Poetica*; Lucretius, *De Rerum Natura*; Ovid, *Metamorphoses;* Plato, *Sophist*; Plutarch, *Moralia*; Quintilian, *Institutio Oratoria*; Tibullus, *Carmina*; Xenophon, *Memorabilia*), all of whom I have translated where appropriate, are to the standard chapter and line numbers as in the Oxford Classical Texts, Loeb Classical Library, and Bibliotheca Scriptorum Graecorum et Romanorum Teubneriana series. Entries in encyclopedias have been cited in text and notes by author's name and volume and page or column of the encyclopedia.

Barber, E. A., ed. *Sexti Properti Carmina*. 2d ed. Oxford: Oxford UP, 1960.

Barsby, John A., ed. and trans. *Ovid's* Amores, *Book One*. Oxford: Oxford UP, 1973.

Brink, C. O., ed. *Horace on Poetry: The 'Ars Poetica'*. Cambridge: Cambridge UP, 1971.

Butler, H. E., ed. and trans. *Propertius*. Cambridge: Harvard UP, 1916.

———, ed. *Sexti Properti Opera Omnia*. London: Constable, 1905.

Butler, H. E., and E. A. Barber, eds. *The Elegies of Propertius*. Oxford: Oxford UP, 1933.

Bywater, Ingram, trans. "Aristotle's *Poetics*." *The Basic Works of Aristotle*. Ed. Richard P. McKeon. New York: Random, 1941. 1455–87.

Carew, Thomas. *The Poems of Thomas Carew with his Masques, Coelum Britannicum*. Ed. Rhodes Dunlap. Oxford: Oxford UP, 1949.

Campion, Thomas. *The Works of Thomas Campion: Complete Songs, Masques, and Treatises with a Selection of the Latin Verse*. Ed. Walter R. Davis. Garden City: Doubleday, 1967.

Camps, W. A., ed. *Propertius: Elegies, Book I*. Cambridge: Cambridge UP, 1961.

———, ed. *Propertius: Elegies, Book II*. Cambridge: Cambridge UP, 1967.

———, ed. *Propertius: Elegies, Book III*. Cambridge: Cambridge UP, 1966.

———, ed. *Propertius: Elegies, Book IV*. 1965. New York: Arno, 1979.

Carrier, Constance, trans. *The Poems of Sextus Propertius*. Bloomington: Indiana UP, 1963.

Dowson, Ernest. *Ernest Dowson 1887–1897: Reminiscences, Unpublished Letters and Marginalia*. Ed. Victor Plarr. New York: Gomme, 1914.

———. *The Poems of Ernest Dowson*. Ed. J. Mark Longaker. Philadelphia: U of Pennsylvania P, 1962.

Enk, P. J., ed. *Sex. Propertii Elegiarum Liber I (Monobiblos)*. 2 vols. Leiden: Brill, 1946.

———., ed. *Sex. Propertii Elegiarum Liber Secundus*. 2 vols. Leiden: Brill, 1962.

Fairbanks, Arthur, ed. and trans. *Philostratus, Imagines; Callistratus, Descriptions*. London: Heinemann, 1931.

Fordyce, C. J. *Catullus: A Commentary*. Oxford: Oxford UP, 1961.

Freud, Sigmund. *The Interpretation of Dreams*. Trans. James Strachey. Vol. 4. London: Hogarth, 1953.

Hanslik, Rudolf, ed. *Sex. Propertii Elegiarum Libri IV*. Stuttgart: Teubner, 1979.

Harmon, A. M., ed. and trans. *Lucian*. 5 vols. Cambridge: Harvard UP, 1913–36.

Hodge, R. I. V., and R. A. Buttimore, eds. *The 'Monobiblos' of Propertius*. Cambridge: Cambridge UP, 1977.

Housman, A. E. *Complete Poems, A. E. Housman*, Centennial Edition. New York: Holt, 1959.

Hubbell, H. M., trans. "The Rhetorica of Philodemus." *Transactions of the Connecticut Academy* (1920): 243–382.

Jensen, Christian, ed. and trans. *Philodemus über die Dichtkunst, funftes Buch.* Dublin: Weidmann, 1973.

Jonson, Ben. *Ben Jonson.* Ed. C. H. Herford, Percy Simpson, and Evelyn Simpson. 11 vols. Oxford: Oxford UP, 1952.

Joyce, James. *A Portrait of the Artist as a Young Man.* New York: Viking, 1916.

———. *Ulysses.* New York: Vintage, 1961.

Kenney, E. J., ed. *P. Ouidi Nasonis Amores, Medicamina Faciei Femineae, Ars Amatoria, Remedia Amoris.* Oxford: Oxford UP, 1965.

Lachmann, Karl, ed. *Sex. Aurelii Propertii Carmina.* 1816. Hildesheim: Olms, 1973.

Lenz, Friedrich, ed. and trans. *Ovid: Die Liebeselegien.* 3d ed. Berlin: Akademie, 1976.

Lessing, G. E. *Laocoon, Nathan the Wise and Minna von Barnheim by Gotthold Ephraim Lessing.* Ed. and trans. W. A. Steele. London: Dent, 1930.

Lowell, Robert. *Day by Day.* London: Faber, 1975; New York: Farrar, 1975.

Lucas, D. W., ed. *Aristotle, Poetics.* 2d ed. Oxford: Oxford UP, 1978.

Milton, John. *The Latin Poems of John Milton.* Ed. Walter McKellar. New Haven: Yale UP, 1930.

Müller, Lucian, ed. *Sex. Propertii Elegiae.* Leipzig: Teubner, 1898.

Paton, W. R., ed. and trans. *The Greek Anthology.* Vol. 1. Cambridge: Harvard UP; London: Heinemann, 1916–18.

Pfeiffer, Rudolf, ed. *Callimachus.* 2 vols. Oxford: Oxford UP, 1949.

Phillimore, John S., ed. *Sexti Properti Carmina.* Oxford: Oxford UP, 1901.

Postgate, J. P., ed. *Select Elegies of Propertius.* London: Macmillan, 1905.

Pound, Ezra. *The Letters of Ezra Pound 1907–1941.* Ed. D. D. Paige. New York: Harcourt, 1950.

———. *Personae: The Collected Shorter Poems of Ezra Pound.* New York: New Directions, 1926; *Collected Shorter Poems.* London: Faber, 1952.

Quinn, Kenneth F., ed. *Catullus: The Poems*. 2d ed. London: Macmillan, 1973.

Richardson, L., Jr., ed. *Propertius: Elegies, I–IV*. Norman: U of Oklahoma P, 1977.

Richmond, Oliffe Lech, ed. *Sexti Properti Quae Supersunt Opera*. Cambridge: Cambridge UP, 1928.

Rothstein, Max, ed. *Die Elegien des Sextus Properz*. 2d ed. 1920, 1924. New York: Garland, 1979.

Stanford, W. B., ed. *Aristophanes: The Frogs*. 2d ed. Basingstoke: Macmillan, 1968.

Thomson, D. F. S., ed. *Catullus: A Critical Edition*. Chapel Hill: U of North Carolina P, 1978.

Wickham, Eduard, and H. W. Garrod, eds. *Q. Horati Flacci Opera*. 2d ed. Oxford: Oxford UP, 1906.

Secondary Sources

Aiken, Pauline. *The Influence of the Latin Elegists on English Lyric Poetry, 1600–1650: With Particular Reference to the Works of Robert Herrick*. Orono: U of Maine P, 1932.

Alfonsi, Luigi. *L'elegia di Properzio*. 1945. New York: Garland, 1979.

Allen, A. W. "Mythological Examples in Propertius." *Proceedings of the American Philological Association* 70 (1939): xxviii–xxix.

———. "'Sincerity' and the Roman Elegists." *Classical Philology* 45 (1950): 145–60.

———. "Sunt Qui Propertium Malint." *Critical Essays on Roman Literature*. Ed. J. P. Sullivan. London: Routledge, 1962. 107–48.

Arnott, Geoffrey. "The Modernity of Menander." *Greece and Rome* 22 (1975): 140–55.

Atkins, J. W. H. *Criticism in Antiquity: A Sketch of its Development*. 2 vols. Cambridge: Cambridge UP, 1934.

Baca, Albert R. "Propertian Elements in the *Cinthia* of Aeneas Silvius Piccolomini." *Classical Journal* 67 (1972–73): 221–26.

Bailey, D. R. Shackleton. *Propertiana*. 1956. Amsterdam: Hakkert, 1967.

———. "Some Recent Experiments in Propertian Criticism." *Proceedings of the Cambridge Philological Society* 182 (1952–53): 9–20.

Baker, R. J. "Beauty and the Beast in Propertius I.3." *Studies in Latin Literature and Roman History* 2 (1980): 245–58.

———. "*Laus in Amore Mori*: Love and Death in Propertius." *Latomus* 29 (1970): 670–98.

Baldi, R. "Carducci e Properzio." *Il mondo classico* 2 (1932): 294–97.

Bartholomé, H. *Ovid und die antike Kunst*. Borna-Leipzig: Noske, 1935.

Bassett, S. E. *The Poetry of Homer*. Berkeley: U of California P, 1938.

Benediktson, D. Thomas. "Catullus 58 B Defended." *Mnemosyne* 39 (1986): 305–12.

———. "Pictorial Art and Ovid's *Amores*." *Quaderni urbinati di cultura classica* 20 (1985): 111–20.

———. "Propertius' 'Elegiacization' of Homer." *Maia* 37 (1985): 17–26.

Bergson, Henri. *The Philosophy of Poetry: The Genius of Lucretius*. Ed. Wade Baskin. New York: Polyglot, 1959.

———. "Understanding Reality." Trans. T. E. Hulme. In *The Stream of Consciousness Technique in the Modern Novel*. Ed. Erwin R. Steinberg. Port Washington: Kennikat, 1979. 50–56.

Birt, Th. "Die vatikanische Ariadne und die dritte Elegie des Properz." *Rheinisches Museum* 50 (1895): 31–65, 161–90.

Bishop, J. David. "Catullus 76: Elegie or Epigram?" *Classical Philology* 67 (1972): 293–94.

Boucher, Jean-Paul. *Études sur Properce: Problèmes d'inspiration et d'art*. 2d ed. Paris: de Boccard, 1965.

Bowling, Lawrence Edward. "What Is the Stream of Consciousness Technique?" *Proceedings of the Modern Language Association* 65 (1950): 333–45.

Boyancé, Pierre L. "Properce." *L'Influence grecque sur la poesie latine de Catulle à Ovide*. Ed. Jean Bayet. Berne: Entretiens Hardt, 1956. 172–93.

———. "Surcharges de rédaction chez Properce." *Revue des études latines* 20 (1942): 54–69.

Bright, David F. *Haec Mihi Fingebam: Tibullus in his World*. Leyden: Brill, 1978.

Brooke-Rose, Christine. *A Structural Analysis of Pound's Usura Canto: Jakobson's Method Extended and Applied to Free Verse*. The Hague: Mouton, 1976.

Buffa, M. Franca. "Interpretazione di Properzio II 34, 61–94." *Civiltà classica e cristiana* 3 (1982): 191–201.

Butrica, James L. *The Manuscript Tradition of Propertius*. Toronto: U of Toronto P, 1984.

———. "Propertius 3.6." *Écho du monde classique* 27 (1983): 17–37.

Cairns, Francis. *Tibullus: A Hellenistic Poet at Rome*. Cambridge: Cambridge UP, 1979.

———. "Two Unidentified Komoi of Propertius I, 3 and II, 29." *Emerita* 45 (1977): 325–53.

Canter, H. V. "The Mythological Paradigm in Greek and Latin Poetry." *American Journal of Philology* 54 (1933): 201–24.

Carter, J. M. "Propertius 2.34C." *Liverpool Classical Monthly* 1 (1976): 41–44.

Coffman, Stanley K. *Imagism: A Chapter for the History of Modern Poetry*. Norman: U of Oklahoma P, 1951.

Copley, Frank O. "Emotional Conflict and its Significance in the Lesbia-poems of Catullus." *American Journal of Philology* 70 (1949): 22–40.

Croce, Benedetto. "Il Benda e Properzio." *Critica* 3 (1947): 88–89.

———. *Poesia antica e moderna*. Bari: Laterza, 1943.

Crowley, Cornelius Joseph. "Echoes of Propertius in the Troilus of Albert of Stade." *Romanitas* 6–7 (1965): 83–89.

Cunningham, J. V. "Campion and Propertius." *Philological Quarterly* 31 (1952): 96.

Curran, Leo C. "Vision and Reality in Propertius 1.3." *Yale Classical Studies* 19 (1966): 189–207.

Damon, P. W., and W. C. Helmbold. "The Structure of Propertius, Book II." *University of California Studies in Classical Philology* 14 (1952): 215–53.

Day, A. A. *The Origins of Latin Love-Elegy*. Oxford: Oxford UP, 1938.

Dilthey, K. "Über zwei Gemälde des Aristides." *Rheinisches Museum* 25 (1870): 151–58.

Disch, H. *De Poetis Aevi Augusti Epicureis*. Nürnberg: Hilz, 1921.

Duff, J. Wright. *A Literary History of Rome: From the Origins to the Close of the Golden Age*. Ed. Adam M. Duff. New York: Barnes, 1959.

Endres, Clifford, and Barbara K. Gold. "Joannes Secundus and his Roman Models: Shapes of Imitation in Renaissance Poetry." *Renaissance Quarterly* 35 (1982): 577–89.

Evans, B. Ifor. *Tradition and Romanticism: Studies in English Poetry from Chaucer to W. B. Yeats*. Hamden: Archon, 1968.

Fantazzi, Charles. "Vergilian Pastoral and Roman Love Elegy." *American Journal of Philology* 87 (1966): 171–91.

Fedeli, Paolo. "Properzio I, 3, interpretazione e proposte sull'origine dell'elegia latina." *Museum Helveticum* 31 (1974): 23–41.

Feder, L. *Ancient Myth in Modern Poetry*. Princeton: Princeton UP, 1970.

Fein, Richard J. *Robert Lowell*. 2d ed. Boston: Twayne, 1979.

Forbes, Clarence A. "Ezra Pound and Sextus Propertius." *Classical Journal* 42 (1946–47): 177–79.

Friedman, Melvin J. *Stream of Consciousness: A Study in Literary Method*. New Haven: Yale UP, 1955.

Gifford, Don, and Robert J. Seidman. *Notes for Joyce: An Annotation of James Joyce's* Ulysses. New York: Dutton, 1974.

Godolphin, F. R. B. "The Unity of Certain Elegies of Propertius." *American Journal of Philology* 55 (1934): 62–66.

Gow, A. S. F. *A. E. Housman: A Sketch*. Cambridge: Cambridge UP, 1936.

Graves, Robert. "Dr. Syntax and Mr. Pound." *The Crowning Privilege*. London: Cassell, 1955. 212–24.

Greenberg, Nathan A. "Metathesis as an Instrument in the Criticism of Poetry." *Transactions of the American Philological Association* 89 (1958): 262–70.

———. "The Poetic Theory of Philodemus." *Harvard Studies in Classical Philology* 62 (1957): 146–48.

Grube, G. M. A. *The Greek and Roman Critics*. London: Methuen, 1965.

Guillemin, A. "L'Élément humain dans l'élégie latine." *Revue des études latines* 18 (1940): 95–111.

Harmon, Daniel P. "Myth and Fantasy in Propertius 1.3." *Transactions of the American Philological Association* 104 (1974): 151–65.

Harrauer, Hermann. *Bibliography to Propertius*. Hildesheim: Gerstenberg, 1973.

Harrington, K. P. "Propertius as a Lover of Nature." *Transactions of the American Philological Association* 32 (1901): xx–xxii.

Helbig, Wolfgang. *Untersuchungen über die campanischen Wandmalerei*. Leipzig: Breitkopf und Hürtel, 1873.

Herrmann, Léon. "Lynceus." *Giornale italiano di filologia* 20 (1967): 139–45.

Hesse, E., ed. Introduction. *New Approaches to Ezra Pound: A Coordinated Investigation of Pound's Poetry and Ideas*. Berkeley: U of California P, 1969. 13–53.

Housman, A. E. *The Classical Papers of A. E. Housman*. Ed. J. Diggle and F. R. D. Goodyear. 3 vols. Cambridge: Cambridge UP, 1972.

Hubbard, Margaret. *Propertius*. London: Duckworth, 1974.

Hubbard, Thomas K. "Art and Vision in Propertius 2.31/32." *Transactions of the American Philological Association* 114 (1984): 281–97.

Humphrey, Robert. *Stream of Consciousness in the Modern Novel*. Berkeley: U of California P, 1954.

Jachmann, Günter. "Ein Elegie des Properz. Ein Überlieferungsschicksal." *Rheinisches Museum* 84 (1935): 193–240.

Kenney, E. J. *Lucretius*. Oxford: Oxford UP, 1977.

Keyssner, Karl. "Die bildende Kunst bei Properz." *Würzburger Festgabe für Heinrich Bulle*. 1938. *Properz*. Ed. Werner Eisenhut. Darmstadt: Wissenschaftliche Buchgesellschaft, 1975. 264–86.

King, Joy K. "Propertius 2.2: A Callimachean 'multum in paruo.'" *Wiener Studien* 94 (1981): 169–84.

———. "Studies in Verbal Repetition in the Monobiblos of Propertius." Diss. U of Colorado, 1969.

Knoche, Ulrich. "Gedanke und Vorschlaege zur Interpretation von Properzens Gedicht 2, 28." *Miscellanea Propertiana. atti dell'accademia Properziana del Subasio*. Assisi: Accademia, 1957. 49–70.

Krókowsky, George. "De Poeta Elegiaco Urbis Amatore." *Eos* 43 (1948–49): 167–85.

Kroll, Wilhelm. "Die Kreuzung der Gattungen." *Studien zum Verständnis der römischen Literatur*. 1924. New York: Garland, 202–24.

Kühn, Josef-Hans. "Die Prooimion-Elegie des zweiten Properz-Buches." *Hermes* 89 (1961): 84–105.

Lacy, Philip H. de. "The Epicurean Analysis of Language." *American Journal of Philology* 60 (1939): 85–92.

Lathrop, Henry B. *Translations from the Classics into English from Caxton to Chapman: 1477–1620*. Madison: U of Wisconsin P, 1933.

Lee, R. W. "*Ut Pictura Poesis*: The Humanistic Theory of Painting." *Art Bulletin* 23 (1940): 197–269.

Lefèvre, Eckard. *Propertius Ludibundus. Elemente des Humors in seinen Elegien*. Heidelberg: Winter, 1966.

———. "L'unità dell'elegia Properziana." *Colloquium Propertianum, atti dell'accademia Properziana del Subasio*. Ed. Marino Bigaroni and Francesco Santucci. Assisi: Accademia, 1977. 25–51.

———. "L'Unité de l'élégie II, 34 de Properce." *L'Élégie romaine: Enracinement—thèmes diffusion, Actes du colloque international organisée par le Faculté des lettres et sciences humaines de Mulhouse*. Ed. Andrée Thill. Paris: Ophrys, 1980. 123–29.

Lesky, Albin. *A History of Greek Literature*. Trans. J. Willis and C. de Heer. 2d ed. New York: Crowell, 1966.

Liddell, Henry G., Robert Scott, Henry S. Jones, and Roderick McKenzie. *A Greek-English Lexicon*. 9th ed. Oxford: Oxford UP, 1940.

Lieberg, Gudo. "L'elegia I 3 di Properzio." *Giornale italiano di filologia* 14 (1961): 308–26.

———. "Die Mythologie des Properz in der Forschung und die Idealisierung Cynthias." *Rheinisches Museum* 112 (1969): 311–47.

Longaker, J. Mark. *Ernest Dowson*. Philadelphia: U of Pennsylvania P, 1945.

Luck, Georg. *The Latin Love Elegy*. 2d ed. Edinburgh: Methuen, 1969.

Lyne, R. O. A. M. "Propertius and Cynthia: Elegy 1.3." *Proceedings of the Cambridge Philological Society* 16 (1970): 60–78.

McEuen, Kathryn A. *Classical Influence upon the Tribe of Ben: A Study of Classical Elements in the Non-Dramatic Poetry of Ben Jonson and His Circle*. New York: Octagon, 1968.

McKeon, Richard P. "Literary Criticism and the Concept of Imitation in Antiquity." *Critics and Criticism: Ancient and Modern*. Ed. R. S. Crane. Chicago: U of Chicago P, 1952. 147–75.

Macleod, C. W. "Propertius 2.26." *Symbolae Osloenses* 5 (1976): 131–36.

Marlow, Norman. *A. E. Housman: Scholar and Poet*. Minneapolis: U of Minnesota P, 1958.

Martini, Edgar. "Ovid und seine Bedeutung für die römische Poesie." *'Επιτύμβιον Heinrich Swoboda dargebracht*. Reichenberg: Stiepel, 1927. 165–94.

Martz, L. L. *The Paradise Within: Studies in Vaughan, Traherne, and Milton*. New Haven: Yale UP, 1964.

Materer, T. *Vortex: Pound, Eliot and Lewis*. Ithaca: Cornell UP, 1979.

Menes, E. P. "The External Evidence for the Division of Propertius, Book 2." *Classical Philology* 78 (1983): 136–44.

Miner, Earl. "Pound, *Haiku*, and the Image." *Hudson Review* 9 (1956–57): 570–84; *Ezra Pound: A Collection of Critical Essays*. Ed. Walter Sutton. Englewood Cliffs: Prentice, 1963. 115–28.

Muecke, Frances. "Mixing of Genres in Augustan Poetry." *Journal of the Australasian Universities Language and Literature Association* 5 (n.d.): 7.1–7.13.

Muscetta, G., ed. *La letteratura italiana, storia e testi.* 10 vols. Bari: Laterza, 1970–80.

Nethercut, William R. "Recent Scholarship on Propertius." *Der Aufstieg und Niedergang der römischen Welt.* 2:30.3 (1983): 1813–57.

Orsini, Gian N. *Benedetto Croce: Philosopher of Art and Literary Critic.* Carbondale: Southern Illinois UP, 1961.

Otto, A. "De Fabulis Propertianis: Particula Prior." Diss. U of Breslau, 1880.

———. "De Fabulis Propertianis: Particula II." *Program des königlichen katholischen Gymnasiums zu Gross-Glochau* 171 (1886): 3–21.

Papanghelis, Theodore D. *Propertius: A Hellenistic Poet on Love and Death.* Cambridge: Cambridge UP, 1987.

Paparelli, Gioacchino. "Enea Silvio Piccolomini, poeta d'amore." *Helikon* 4 (1964): 253–60.

Parker, Douglass. "The Ovidian Coda." *Arion* 8 (1969): 80–97.

Pasoli, Elio. "Poesia d'amore e metapoesia, aspetti della modernità di Properzio." *Colloquium Propertianum, atti dell'Accademia Properziana del Subasio.* Ed. Marino Bigaroni and Francesco Santucci. Assisi: Accademia, 1977. 101–21.

Pasquali, Giorgio. "Croce e le letterature classiche." *Leonardo* 8 (1937): 45–50.

Pauly, August von. *Paulys Realencyclopädia der klassischen Altertumswissenschaft.* 58 vols. Munich: Druckenmüller, 1893–1980.

Penna, Antonio La. *L'integrazione difficile, un profilo di Properzio.* Turin: Einaudi, 1977.

———. *Properzio, saggio critico seguito da due ricerche filologiche.* Florence: Nova Italia, 1951.

Porter, David H. "Ring-composition in Classical Literature and Contemporary Music." *Classical World* 65 (1971): 1–8.

Pound, E. "Mr. Housman at Little Bethel." *Criterion* 13 (1934): 216–24.

Quinn, Kenneth F. *Latin Explorations: Critical Studies in Roman Literature.* London: Routledge, 1963.

Reitzenstein, R. "Properz-Studien." *Hermes* 31 (1896): 185–220.

Renz, H. *Mythologische Beispiele in Ovids erotischer Elegie* Würzburg: Triltsch, 1935.

Richmond, Oliffe Lech. "The Archetype of Propertius and his Scheme of Composition." *Proceedings of the Cambridge Philological Society* (1911): 6–8.

———. "Towards a Reconstruction of the Text of Propertius." *Classical Quarterly* 12 (1918): 59–75.

Robathan, D. M. "Cristoforo Landino's Use of Propertius." *Transactions of the American Philological Association* 78 (1947): 434.

Robinson, Alan. *Symbol to Vortex: Poetry, Painting and Ideas, 1885–1914.* New York: St. Martin's, 1985.

Romizi, A. *Le fonti latine dell'*Orlando Furioso. Turin: Paravia, 1896.

Roscher, Wilhelm H. *Ausfürliches Lexikon der griechischen und römischen Mythologie.* 10 vols. 1884–1937. Hildesheim: Olms, 1965.

Ross, David O., Jr. *Gallus, Elegy and Rome.* Cambridge: Cambridge UP, 1975.

Rostagni, Augosto. "Sulle tracce di un'estetica dell'intuizione presso gli antichi." *Atene e Roma* 1 (1920): 46–57.

Rudd, Niall. "Theme and Imagery in Propertius 2. 15." *Classical Quarterly* 32 (1982): 152–55.

Sabbadini, Remigio. "L'elegia prima del libro primo di Properzio." *Atene e Roma* 2 (1899): 26–29.

Sadler, Lynn V. *Thomas Carew.* Boston: Twayne, 1979.

Scafoglio, Domenico. *Vincenzo Padula, storia di una censura.* Cosenza: Lerici, 1979.

Schöne, W. "De Ratione Properti Fabulas Adhibendi." Diss. U of Leipzig, 1911.

Skutsch, O. "The Second Book of Propertius." *Harvard Studies in Classical Philology* 79 (1975): 229–33.

———. "The Structure of the Propertian *Monobiblos.*" *Classical Philology* 58 (1963): 238–39.

Stahl, Hans Peter. *Propertius: "Love" and "War".* Berkeley: U of California P, 1985.

Stanford, W. B. *The Sound of Greek: Studies in the Greek Theory and Practice of Euphony.* Berkeley: U of California P, 1967.

Stenico, Arturo. *Roman and Etruscan Painting.* Trans. Angus Malcolm. New York: Viking, 1963.

Suits, Thomas A. "Mythology, Address, and Structure in Propertius 2.8." *Transactions of the American Philological Association* 96 (1965): 427–37.

Sullivan, J. P. "Ezra Pound and the Classics." *New Approaches to Ezra Pound: A Coordinated Investigation of Pound's Poetry and Ideas.* Ed. E. Hesse. Berkeley: U of California P. 215–41.

———. *Ezra Pound and Sextus Propertius: A Study in Creative Translation.* Austin: U of Texas P, 1964.

———. "The Poet as Translator: Ezra Pound and Sextus Propertius." *Kenyon Review* 23 (1961): 462–81.

———. "Pound's Homage to Propertius: The Structure of a Mask." *Essays in Criticism* 10 (1960): 239–49.

———. *Propertius: A Critical Introduction.* Cambridge: Cambridge UP, 1976.

———. "Propertius 2.29.38." *Classical Quarterly* 11 (1961): 1–2.

———., ed. *Critical Essays on Roman Literature: Elegy and Lyric.* London: Routledge, 1962.

Swann, Thomas B. *Ernest Dowson.* New York: Twayne, 1964.

Tait, Jane I. M. "Philodemus' Influence on the Latin Poets." Diss. Bryn Mawr U, 1941.

Tartari Chersoni, Marinella. "Properzio II 14, per una interpretazione unitaria del testo." *Giornale italiano di filologia* 31 (1979): 66–80.

Thomas, Richard F. "New Comedy, Callimachus, and Roman Elegy." *Harvard Studies in Classical Philology* 83 (1979): 179–206.

Tomaszuk, Valeri. *A Romantic Interpretation of Propertius: Vincenzo Padula.* Aquila: Japadre, 1971.

Ton, J. del. Rev. of *La fortuna letteraria di Properzio*, by A. Fortini. *Latinitas* 4 (1956): 305.

Townend, Gavin. "Imagery in Lucretius." *Lucretius.* Ed. D. R. Dudley. New York: Basic Books, 1965. 95–114.

Tränkle, Hermann. *Die Sprachkunst des Properz und die Tradition der lateinischen Dichtersprache, Hermes* Einzelschrift 15. Wiesbaden: Steiner, 1960.

Ullman, B. L. "The Manuscripts of Propertius." *Classical Philology* 6 (1911): 282–301.

———. *Studies in the Italian Renaissance.* 2d ed. Rome: Storia e letteratura, 1973.

Veremans, Joseph. "Le Thème élégiaque de la *vita iners* chez Tibulle et Properce," in *Hommages à Robert Schilling.* Ed. H. Zehnacker and G. Hentz. Paris: Societé d'édition les belles lettres, 1983. 423–36.

Vessey, D. W. T. C. "Nescio Quid Maius." *Proceedings of the Vergilian Society* 9 (1969–70): 53–76.

Walker, Steven F. *Theocritus*. Boston: Twayne, 1970.

Warden, John. *Fallax Opus: Poet and Reader in the Elegies of Propertius*. Toronto: U of Toronto P, 1980.

Weinberg, Bernard. "Castelvetro's Theory of Poetics." *Critics and Criticism: Ancient and Modern*. Ed. R. S. Crane. Chicago: U of Chicago P, 1952. 349–71.

West, Michael. "Prothalamia in Propertius and Spenser." *Comparative Literature* 26 (1974): 346–53.

White, Ronald E. "Dramatic Unity in Propertius 1.8, 2.29, 2.33." *Classical Philology* 56 (1961): 217–29.

———. "The Structure of Propertius 2.28: Dramatic Unity." *Transactions of the American Philological Association* 89 (1958): 254–61.

———. "The Unity of Propertius 2.34 and 3.20." *Laudatores Temporis Acti: Studies in Memory of Wallace Everett Caldwell*. Ed. Mary F. Gyles and Eugene W. Davis. Chapel Hill: U of North Carolina P, 1969. 63–72.

Whitman, Cedric H. *Homer and the Homeric Tradition*. Cambridge: Harvard UP, 1967.

Wiggers, Nancy. "Variations on a Theme: Nightmare and Daydream in Propertius II. 26." *Latomus* 39 (1980): 121–28.

Wilkinson, L. P. "Philodemus and Poetry." *Greece and Rome* 2 (1932–33): 144–51.

Williams, Gordon. *Figures of Thought in Roman Poetry*. New Haven: Yale UP, 1980.

———. *Tradition and Originality in Roman Poetry*. Oxford: Oxford UP, 1968.

Wimmel, Walter. *Kallimachus in Rom. Die Nachfolge seines apologetischen Dichtens in der Augusteerzeit, Hermes* Einzelschrift 16. Wiesbaden: Steiner, 1960.

Windelband, W. *A History of Philosophy*. Trans. J. H. Tufts. 2d ed. 2 vols. New York: Macmillan, 1901.

Winters, Yvor. *The Function of Criticism*. Denver: Swallow, 1957.

———. "Poetic Styles, Old and New." *Four Poets on Poetry*. Ed. Don C. Allen. Baltimore: Johns Hopkins UP, 1959. 44–75.

Woolf, Virginia. "Modern Fiction." *The Common Reader: First Series*. London: Hogarth, 1925. 184–95.

Yardley, J. C. "Comic Influences in Propertius." *Phoenix* 26 (1972): 134–39.

Ziegler, Konrat, and Walther Sontheimer. *Der Kleine Pauly*. 5 vols. Stuttgart: Druckenmüller, 1964–75.

Zingerle, Anton. "Petrarcha's Verhältnis zu den römischen Dichtern." *Kleine philologische Abhandlungen*. Innsbruck: Wagner'sche, 1871–87. 1: 5–21.

Index

D. Thomas Benediktson is an associate professor of classics and comparative literature at The University of Tulsa, where he won the Distinguished Teacher Award in 1987. He holds A.B. and M.A. degrees in rhetoric from the University of California, Berkeley, and M.A. and Ph.D. degrees in classics from The University of Texas at Austin. Professor Benediktson has articles and book reviews, both published and forthcoming, on Greek and Roman poetry and on ancient aesthetic theory in *Phoenix, Maia, Quaderni urbinati di cultura classica, Mnemosyne,* and *Classical World.* He has also delivered papers on Roman poetry and on the Roman emperor Caligula. He lives in Tulsa, Oklahoma, with his wife and two sons.